The Most Holy

This Memorial Edition copy donated by:

_____

In Loving Memory of:

_____

who resided in:

_____

Please pray for the resting of their soul.

Thank You and May God Bless You.

What are Memorial Edition copies?

Memorial Editions of <u>The Most Holy Rosary</u> are copies that provide you with the opportunity to write in the name of a family member, friend, or stranger who has passed away, while also requesting that the reader pray for the resting of your family member or friend's soul.

Regular price Memorial Edition copies are for sale on amazon's websites in the United States, the United Kingdom, Germany, France, Italy, and Spain.

However, we want people to pray the Rosary, and we encourage people to pray for the souls of the deceased, especially for our loved ones.

So, we are offering lower cost books available to you.

Discounted copies of Memorial Editions are available at Great Point Publishing for a lower cost per book, while being able to order multiple copies at one time.

To order lower cost discounted copies please visit:

greatpointpublishing.com/rosary

We hope you enjoy the opportunity to give a copy of this book as a present to a friend, or family member, or leave it in a Church as a gift for anyone to take.

Together let's promote the Rosary.

Together let's change the world.

Thank you.

The Most Holy Rosary

Pray the Rosary Easily, Any Day this Week

Christopher Hallenbeck

Great Point Publishing

Gloversville, NY

The Most Holy Rosary
Pray the Rosary Easily, Any Day this Week
- Christopher Hallenbeck

Copyright © 2020 Christopher Hallenbeck, Great Point Publishing, LLC. ALL RIGHTS RESERVED. No part of this book may be reproduced, stored in a retrieval system, or transmitted by any means without the written permission of the author.

Cover design by: Gareth Bobowski

Book design by: Christopher Hallenbeck

Front Cover Royalty Free Image of Mary:
"Photo 107885056 © Nuiiko | Dreamstime.com"

Front and Back Cover of Our Lady of Mount Carmel Church, in Gloversville, NY, drawn by Frank Morgan from Troy, NY.

To order additional copies of this title, contact your favorite local bookstore or visit *www.greatpointpublishing.com/store*

For Wholesale Inquiry and Volume Discount pricing visit *www.greatpointpublishing.com/wholesale*

Paperback ISBN: 978-1-7333797-7-9

Printed in the United States of America

Published by: ***Great Point Publishing, LLC.***
Gloversville, NY

Dedication:

There are two organizations at The Church of the Holy Spirit in Gloversville, NY, that I have had the good fortune to experience active membership in. In turn, they have brought along many incredible experiences and blessings to my life, as well as many new friendships, both locally and nationally.

With that being said, I'd like to dedicate this book to all of you who are members of the Knights of Columbus, and also to those who continue to keep the faith, and who keep watch through attending Adoration of The Blessed Sacrament.

Thank you to all of you who I know locally through my involvement in the Knights of Columbus and at the Perpetual Eucharistic Adoration Chapel, and thank you also, to anyone reading this who helps create these same opportunities and experiences in your own individual hometowns and parishes.

TABLE OF CONTENTS

Introduction	1
The 15 Promises of Mary to Christians who Pray The Rosary	2
The Most Holy Rosary	4
Sunday and Wednesday– The Glorious Mysteries	5
Monday and Saturday – The Joyful Mysteries	22
Tuesday and Friday – The Sorrowful Mysteries	39
Thursday – The Luminous Mysteries	56
An Inspirational Rosary Novena Story from Gloversville, NY	73
About Frank Morgan	92
About The Author	101
Thanks and Acknowledgements	101
A small request	101
End Notes	102

INTRODUCTION

This book was written to help you pray the Holy Rosary easily. If you're just discovering the Rosary for the first time, then this book will be a simple but informative introduction to the Rosary, and also help you learn how to pray the Rosary.

For the more experienced devotees of the Rosary who may prefer to pray the mysteries on the days that they are traditionally associated with, this book will provide you with a resource to aid you in your daily prayer routine, along with providing a helpful tool to use when you introduce the Rosary to new audiences.

Next, let's look at some of the ways this book can help both new and experienced friends of the Rosary. Here is a brief outline of highlights featured in this book and how they can help you:

- The 15 Promises of Mary to Christians who pray the Rosary are included on the next two pages as a source of inspiration and reminder for reasons to pray the Rosary.

- This book includes the Rosary Mystery prayers for all 7 days in the week, so you can pray them any day this week.

- Also included for each set of mysteries for the daily Rosary, is a step by step image on how to pray the Rosary.

- The individual prayers for all five mysteries of the Rosary are written out for you every single day. Each mystery also features a specific image to help you learn and remember all of the mysteries easier.

- At the end of the book is an inspirational Rosary Novena story that I hope you enjoy reading and find inspiring also.

In conclusion, thank you for praying the rosary, and finally...

"Together, let's promote the rosary.
Together, let's change the world."

-Christopher Hallenbeck
Gloversville, NY
October 4, 2020

THE 15 PROMISES OF MARY TO CHRISTIANS
WHO PRAY THE ROSARY

Made by the Blessed Virgin to St. Dominic and Blessed Alanus.

1. To all those who will recite my Rosary devoutly, I promise my special protection and very great graces.

2. Those who will persevere in the recitation of my Rosary shall receive some signal grace.

3. The Rosary shall be a very powerful armor against hell; it shall destroy vice, deliver from sin, and shall dispel heresy.

4. The Rosary shall make virtue and good works flourish, and shall obtain for souls the most abundant divine mercies; it shall substitute in hearts love of God for love of the world, elevate them to desire heavenly and eternal goods. Oh, that souls would sanctify themselves by this means!

5. "Those who trust themselves to me through the Rosary, shall not perish.

6. Those who will recite my Rosary piously, considering its Mysteries, shall not be overwhelmed by misfortune nor die a bad death. The sinner shall be converted; the just shall grow in grace and become worthy of eternal life.

7. Those truly devoted to my Rosary shall not die without the consolations of the Church, or without grace.

8. Those who will recite my Rosary shall find during their life and at their death the light of God, the fulness of His grace, and shall share in the merits of the blessed.

9. I will deliver very promptly from purgatory the souls devoted to my Rosary.

10. The true children of my Rosary shall enjoy great glory in heaven.

11. *What you ask through my Rosary, you shall obtain.*

12. Those who propagate my Rosary shall obtain through me aid in all their necessities.

13. I have obtained from my Son that all the confreres of the Rosary shall have for their brethren in life and death the saints of Heaven.

14. Those who recite my Rosary faithfully are all my beloved children, the brothers and sisters of Jesus Christ.

15. Devotion to my Rosary is a special sign of predestination.

The Most Holy Rosary

SUNDAY & WEDNESDAY

Photo Courtesy of: Esther Gefroh

The Glorious Mysteries

HOW TO PRAY THE ROSARY

The image on the next page, and the steps below will show you how to pray the Rosary and also display the steps on a set of rosary beads*. These steps are just an overview. They are presented in order, and in more detail for each of the days that follow in the Rosary. The individual prayers for are also written out for you in the pages that follow for the Rosary.

Note: The image of the rosary that shows these steps on rosary beads were used with permission from The Rosary Foundation at www.erosary.com

HOW TO PRAY THE ROSARY STEPS

1. Make the Sign of The Cross and Say The Apostle's Creed.
2. Say one Our Father Prayer.
3. Say three Hail Mary Prayers.
4. Say one Glory Be To The Father Prayer.
5. Say one Fatima Prayer.
6. Announce the First Mystery and Say one Our Father prayer.
7. Say ten consecutive Hail Mary prayers; meditate on the first mystery as you are praying.
8. Say one Glory Be To The Father Prayer.
9. Say one Fatima Prayer.
10. Repeat steps 7, 8, and 9 for the second, third, fourth and fifth mysteries of The Rosary.
11. Say one Hail Holy Queen Prayer.
12. Make The Sign of The Cross

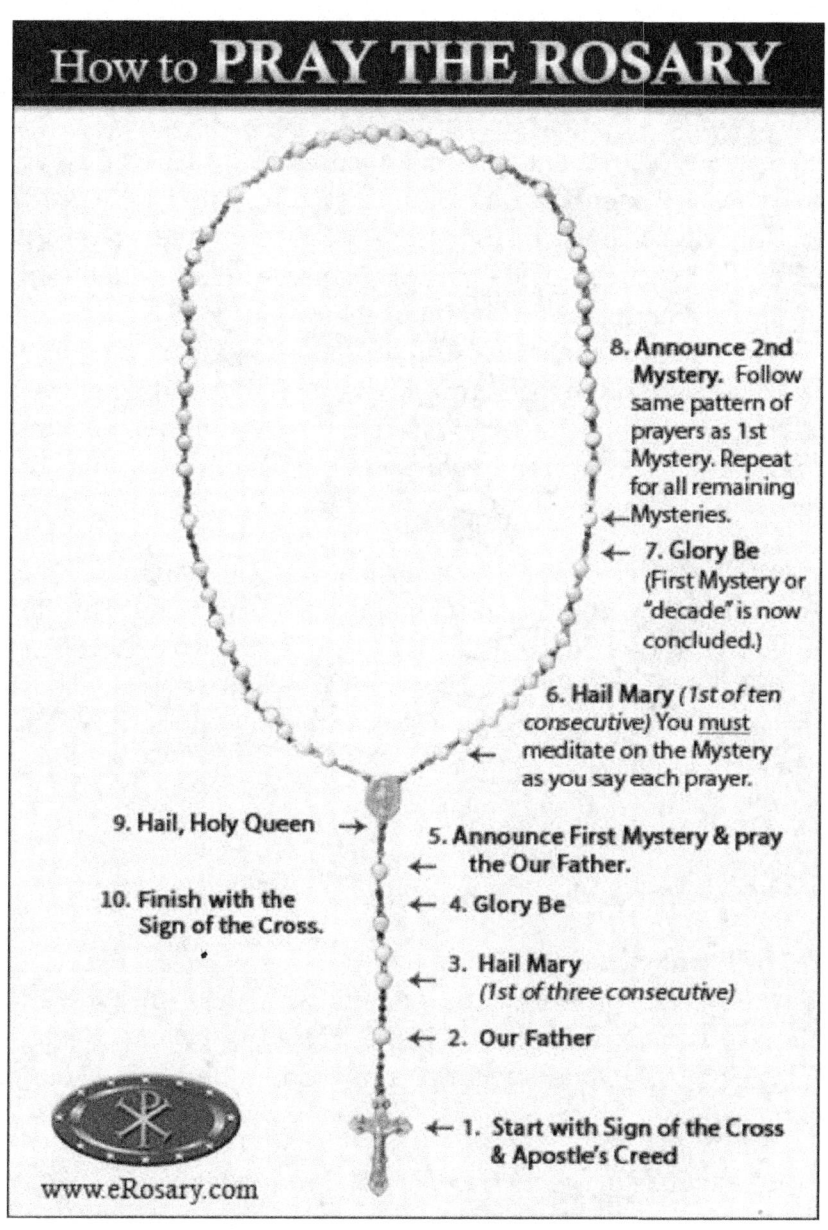

Image Courtesy of Dan Rudden at The Rosary Foundation.

The Most Holy Rosary

The Apostle's Creed
I believe in God, the Father Almighty, Creator of Heaven and Earth; and in Jesus Christ, His only Son, Our Lord, Who was conceived by the Holy Spirit, born of the Virgin Mary, suffered under Pontius Pilate, was crucified, died, and was buried. He descended into Hell. The third day He arose again from the dead; He ascended into Heaven, sitteth at the right hand of God, the Father Almighty; from thence He shall come to judge the living and the dead. I believe in the Holy Spirit, the holy Catholic Church, the communion of saints, the forgiveness of sins, the resurrection of the body, and the life everlasting. Amen.

(1) Our Father
Our Father, Who art in Heaven, hallowed be Thy name; Thy kingdom come; Thy will be done on Earth as it is in Heaven. Give us this day our daily bread; and forgive us our trespasses as we forgive those who trespass against us; and lead us not into temptation, but deliver us from evil. Amen.

The 3 Hail Mary beads

For an increase in the virtue of faith...I humbly pray:

(1) Hail Mary
Hail Mary, full of grace. The Lord is with thee. Blessed art thou amongst women, and blessed is the fruit of thy womb, Jesus. Holy Mary, Mother of God, pray for us sinners, now and at the hour of our death. Amen.

For an increase in the virtue of hope...I humbly pray:

(1) Hail Mary
Hail Mary, full of grace. The Lord is with thee. Blessed art thou amongst women, and blessed is the fruit of thy womb, Jesus. Holy Mary, Mother of God, pray for us sinners, now and at the hour of our death. Amen.

For an increase in the virtue of charity…I humbly pray:

(1) Hail Mary
Hail Mary, full of grace. The Lord is with thee. Blessed art thou amongst women, and blessed is the fruit of thy womb, Jesus. Holy Mary, Mother of God, pray for us sinners, now and at the hour of our death. Amen.

(1) Glory Be
Glory be to the Father, and to the Son, and to the Holy Spirit, as it was in the beginning, is now, and ever shall be, world without end. Amen.

(1) Oh my Jesus
Oh my Jesus, forgive us our sins, save us from the fires of hell and lead all souls into heaven, especially those in most need of thy mercy. Amen.

THE FIRST GLORIOUS MYSTERY

THE RESURRECTION

O glorious Mother Mary, meditating on the Mystery of the Resurrection of Our Lord from the Dead, which we read in Matthew 28: 1-10; Mark 16: 1-18; Luke 24: 1-49; and John 20:1-29, when on the morning of the third day after His death and burial, Jesus arose from the dead and appeared to thee, Blessed Mother, and filled thy heart with unspeakable joy; then appeared to the holy women, and to His disciples, who adored Him as their risen God.

Meditating on Mystery of the Resurrection of Our Lord from the Dead and praying for an increase in the virtue of Faith I humbly pray...

(1) Our Father

Our Father, Who art in Heaven, hallowed be Thy name; Thy kingdom come; Thy will be done on Earth as it is in Heaven. Give us this day our daily bread; and forgive us our trespasses as we forgive those who trespass against us; and lead us not into temptation, but deliver us from evil. Amen.

(10) Hail Mary

Hail Mary, full of grace. The Lord is with thee. Blessed art thou amongst women, and blessed is the fruit of thy womb, Jesus. Holy Mary, Mother of God, pray for us sinners, now and at the hour of our death. Amen.

(1) Glory Be

Glory be to the Father, and to the Son, and to the Holy Spirit, as it was in the beginning, is now, and ever shall be, world without end. Amen.

(1) Oh my Jesus:

Oh my Jesus, forgive us our sins, save us from the fires of hell and lead all souls into heaven, especially those in most need of thy mercy. Amen.

I bind these full blown roses with a petition for the virtue of

FAITH

and humbly lay this bouquet at your feet.

THE SECOND GLORIOUS MYSTERY

THE ASCENSION

O glorious Mother Mary, meditating on the Mystery of the Ascension, which we read in Mark: 16: 19-20; Luke 24: 50-51; and Acts 1: 6-11, when thy divine Son, after forty days on Earth, went to Mount Olivet accompanied by His disciples and thee, where all adored Him for the last time, after which He promised to remain with them until the end of the world; then, extending His pierced hands over all in a last blessing, as ascended before their eyes into heaven.

Meditating on Mystery of the Ascension of Our Lord and praying for an increase in the virtue of Hope...I humbly pray...

(1) Our Father

Our Father, Who art in Heaven, hallowed be Thy name; Thy kingdom come; Thy will be done on Earth as it is in Heaven. Give us this day our daily bread; and forgive us our trespasses as we forgive those who trespass against us; and lead us not into temptation, but deliver us from evil. Amen.

(10) Hail Mary

Hail Mary, full of grace. The Lord is with thee. Blessed art thou amongst women, and blessed is the fruit of thy womb, Jesus. Holy Mary, Mother of God, pray for us sinners, now and at the hour of our death. Amen.

(1) Glory Be

Glory be to the Father, and to the Son, and to the Holy Spirit, as it was in the beginning, is now, and ever shall be, world without end. Amen.

(1) Oh my Jesus:

Oh my Jesus, forgive us our sins, save us from the fires of hell and lead all souls into heaven, especially those in most need of thy mercy. Amen.

I bind these full blown roses with a petition for the virtue of

HOPE

and humbly lay this bouquet at your feet.

THE THIRD GLORIOUS MYSTERY

THE DESCENT OF THE HOLY SPIRIT

O glorious Mother Mary, meditating on the Mystery of the Descent of the Holy Ghost, which we read Acts 2:1-41 when the apostles being assembled with thee in a house in Jerusalem, the Holy Spirit descended upon them in the form of fiery tongues, inflaming the hearts of the apostles with the fire of divine love, teaching them all truths, giving to them the gift of tongues, and, filling thee with the plenitude of His grace, inspired thee to pray for the apostles and the first Christians.

Meditating on Mystery of the descent of The Holy Spirit of Our Lord and praying for an increase in the virtue of Charity…I humbly pray…

(1) Our Father

Our Father, Who art in Heaven, hallowed be Thy name; Thy kingdom come; Thy will be done on Earth as it is in Heaven. Give us this day our daily bread; and forgive us our trespasses as we forgive those who trespass against us; and lead us not into temptation, but deliver us from evil. Amen.

(10) Hail Mary

Hail Mary, full of grace. The Lord is with thee. Blessed art thou amongst women, and blessed is the fruit of thy womb, Jesus. Holy Mary, Mother of God, pray for us sinners, now and at the hour of our death. Amen.

(1) Glory Be

Glory be to the Father, and to the Son, and to the Holy Spirit, as it was in the beginning, is now, and ever shall be, world without end. Amen.

(1) Oh my Jesus:

Oh my Jesus, forgive us our sins, save us from the fires of hell and lead all souls into heaven, especially those in most need of thy mercy. Amen.

I bind these full blown roses with a petition for the virtue of

CHARITY

and humbly lay this bouquet at your feet.

THE FOURTH GLORIOUS MYSTERY

THE ASSUMPTION OF OUR BLESSED MOTHER INTO HEAVEN

O glorious Mother Mary, meditating on the Mystery of Thy Assumption into Heaven, when consumed with the desire to be united with thy divine Son in heaven, thy soul departed from thy body and united itself to Him, Who, out of the excessive love He bore for thee, His Mother, whose virginal body was His first tabernacle, took that body into heaven and there, amidst the acclaims of the angels and saints, reinfused into it thy soul. Meditating on Mystery of The Assumption of Our Blessed Mother into Heaven, which is implied in the book of Revelation 12:1, is taught in The Catechism of the Catholic Church when the Assumption is defined in Sections 966 and 974, and lastly The Assumption is a part of Catholic Tradition…

Meditating on Mystery of The Assumption of Our Blessed Mother into Heaven and praying for an increase in the virtue of Union with Christ...I humbly pray...

(1) Our Father

Our Father, Who art in Heaven, hallowed be Thy name; Thy kingdom come; Thy will be done on Earth as it is in Heaven. Give us this day our daily bread; and forgive us our trespasses as we forgive those who trespass against us; and lead us not into temptation, but deliver us from evil. Amen.

(10) Hail Mary

Hail Mary, full of grace. The Lord is with thee. Blessed art thou amongst women, and blessed is the fruit of thy womb, Jesus. Holy Mary, Mother of God, pray for us sinners, now and at the hour of our death. Amen.

(1) Glory Be

Glory be to the Father, and to the Son, and to the Holy Spirit, as it was in the beginning, is now, and ever shall be, world without end. Amen.

(1) Oh my Jesus:

Oh my Jesus, forgive us our sins, save us from the fires of hell and lead all souls into heaven, especially those in most need of thy mercy. Amen.

I bind these full blown roses with a petition for the virtue of

UNION WITH CHRIST

and humbly lay this bouquet at your feet.

THE FIFTH GLORIOUS MYSTERY

*THE CORONATION OF OUR BLESSED MOTHER
IN HEAVEN AS ITS QUEEN*

O glorious Mother Mary, meditating on the Mystery of Thy Coronation in Heaven which is implied in the book of Revelation 12:1, and also celebrated annually on August 22nd when Catholics celebrate the feast of the Queenship of Mary. O Queen of The Holy Rosary, when upon being taken up to Heaven after thy death, thou wert triply crowned as the August Queen of Heaven. First by God the Father as His beloved Daughter, next by God the Son as His dearest Mother, and finally by God the Holy Ghost as His chaste Spouse, the most perfect adorer of the Blessed Trinity, pleading our cause as our most powerful and merciful Mother.

Meditating on Mystery of The Coronation of Our Blessed Mother in Heaven as its Queen, and praying for an increase in the virtue of Union with Thee, I humbly pray...

(1) Our Father

Our Father, Who art in Heaven, hallowed be Thy name; Thy kingdom come; Thy will be done on Earth as it is in Heaven. Give us this day our daily bread; and forgive us our trespasses as we forgive those who trespass against us; and lead us not into temptation, but deliver us from evil. Amen.

(10) Hail Mary

Hail Mary, full of grace. The Lord is with thee. Blessed art thou amongst women, and blessed is the fruit of thy womb, Jesus. Holy Mary, Mother of God, pray for us sinners, now and at the hour of our death. Amen.

(1) Glory Be

Glory be to the Father, and to the Son, and to the Holy Spirit, as it was in the beginning, is now, and ever shall be, world without end. Amen.

(1) Oh my Jesus:

Oh my Jesus, forgive us our sins, save us from the fires of hell and lead all souls into heaven, especially those in most need of thy mercy. Amen.

I bind these full blown roses with a petition for the virtue of

UNION WITH THEE

and humbly lay this bouquet at your feet.

SPIRITUAL COMMUNION

MY JESUS, really present in the most holy Sacrament of the Altar, since I cannot now receive Thee under the sacramental veil, I beseech Thee, with a heart full of love and longing, to come spiritually into my soul through the immaculate heart of Thy most holy Mother, and abide with me forever; Thou in me, and I in Thee, in time and in eternity, in Mary. Amen.

Hail Holy Queen
Hail, Holy Queen, Mother of mercy, our life, our sweetness and our hope. To thee do we cry, poor banished children of Eve: to thee do we send up our sighs, mourning and weeping in this valley of tears. Turn then, most gracious Advocate, thine eyes of mercy toward us, and after this our exile, show unto us the blessed fruit of thy womb, Jesus. O clement, O loving, O sweet Virgin Mary! Pray for us, O Holy Mother of God... that we may be made worthy of the promises of Christ. Amen

LET US PRAY
O God! Whose only-begotten Son, by His life, death, and resurrection, has purchased for us the reward of eternal life; grant, we beseech Thee, that, meditating upon these mysteries of the Most Holy Rosary of the Blessed Virgin Mary, we may imitate what they contain and obtain what they promise. Through the same Christ our Lord. Amen.

May the divine assistance remain always with us. Amen. And may the souls of the faithful departed, through the mercy *of* God, rest in peace. Amen. Holy Virgin, with thy loving Child, thy blessing give to us this day *(night)*.

Memorare
Remember, O most gracious Virgin Mary, that never was it known that anyone who fled to thy protection, implored thy help or sought thy intercession, was left unaided. Inspired by this confidence, We fly unto thee, O Virgin of virgins my Mother; to thee do we come, before thee we stand, sinful and sorrowful; O Mother of the Word Incarnate,

despise not our petitions, but in thy mercy hear and answer them. Amen.

Saint Michael Prayer
Saint Michael, the Archangel, defend us in battle. Be our protection against the wickedness and snares of the devil. May God rebuke him, we humbly pray; and do thou, O Prince of the heavenly host, by the power of God cast into hell Satan and all the evil spirits who prowl throughout the world seeking the ruin of souls. Amen.

Sign of the Cross
In the name of the Father, and the Son, and the Holy Spirit, Amen.

What Page to Turn to Next:

If today is a Sunday then turn to page 22 to prepare for the Joyful Mysteries tomorrow on Monday.

If today is a Wednesday then turn to page 56 to prepare for the Luminous Mysteries tomorrow on Thursday.

MONDAY & SATURDAY

The Joyful Mysteries

HOW TO PRAY THE ROSARY

The image on the next page, and the steps below will show you how to pray the Rosary and also display the steps on a set of rosary beads*. These steps are just an overview. They are presented in order, and in more detail for each of the days that follow in the Rosary. The individual prayers for are also written out for you in the pages that follow for the Rosary.

Note: The image of the rosary that shows these steps on rosary beads were used with permission from The Rosary Foundation at www.erosary.com

HOW TO PRAY THE ROSARY STEPS

1. Make the Sign of The Cross and Say The Apostle's Creed.
2. Say one Our Father Prayer.
3. Say three Hail Mary Prayers.
4. Say one Glory Be To The Father Prayer.
5. Say one Fatima Prayer.
6. Announce the First Mystery and Say one Our Father prayer.
7. Say ten consecutive Hail Mary prayers; meditate on the first mystery as you are praying.
8. Say one Glory Be To The Father Prayer.
9. Say one Fatima Prayer.
10. Repeat steps 7, 8, and 9 for the second, third, fourth and fifth mysteries of The Rosary.
11. Say one Hail Holy Queen Prayer.
12. Make The Sign of The Cross

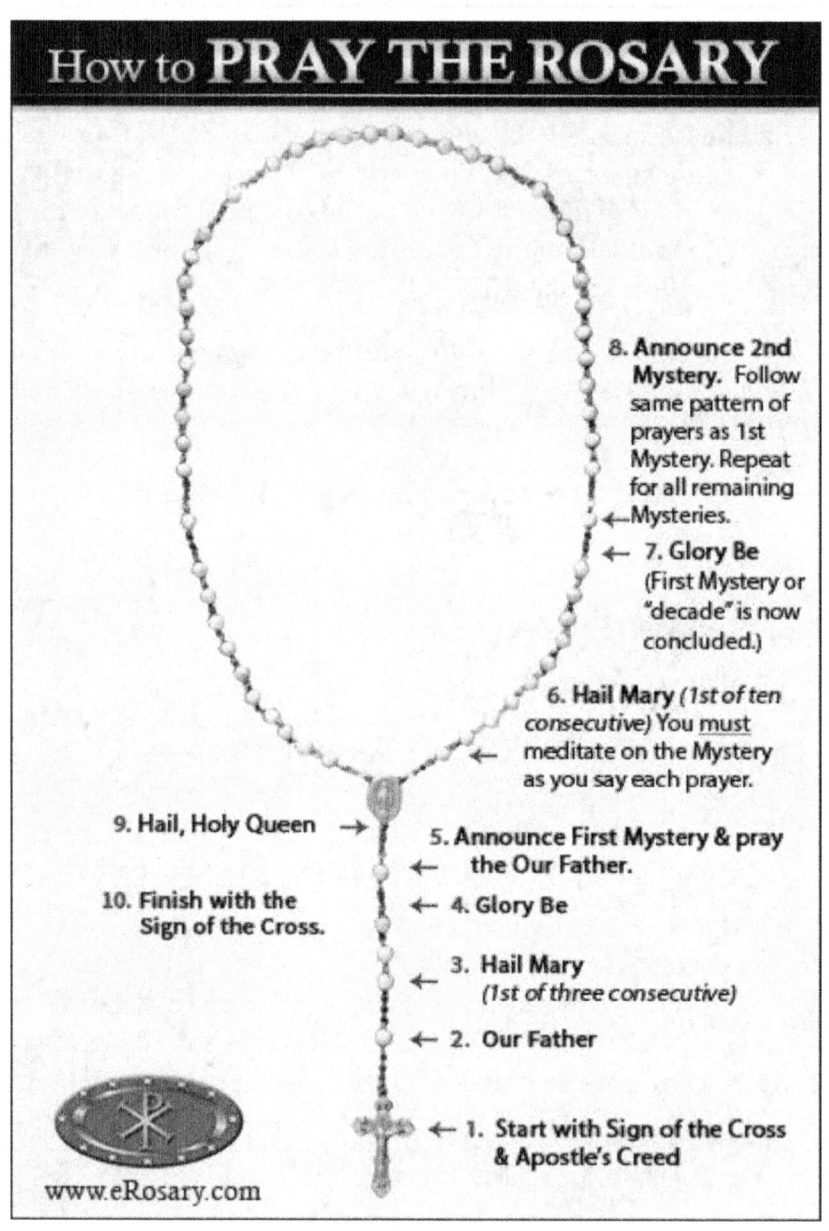

Image Courtesy of Dan Rudden at The Rosary Foundation.

THE MOST HOLY ROSARY

The Apostle's Creed
I believe in God, the Father Almighty, Creator of Heaven and Earth; and in Jesus Christ, His only Son, Our Lord, Who was conceived by the Holy Spirit, born of the Virgin Mary, suffered under Pontius Pilate, was crucified, died, and was buried. He descended into Hell. The third day He arose again from the dead; He ascended into Heaven, sitteth at the right hand of God, the Father Almighty; from thence He shall come to judge the living and the dead. I believe in the Holy Spirit, the holy Catholic Church, the communion of saints, the forgiveness of sins, the resurrection of the body, and the life everlasting. Amen.

(1) Our Father
Our Father, Who art in Heaven, hallowed be Thy name; Thy kingdom come; Thy will be done on Earth as it is in Heaven. Give us this day our daily bread; and forgive us our trespasses as we forgive those who trespass against us; and lead us not into temptation, but deliver us from evil. Amen.

The 3 Hail Mary beads

For an increase in the virtue of faith...I humbly pray:

(1) Hail Mary
Hail Mary, full of grace. The Lord is with thee. Blessed art thou amongst women, and blessed is the fruit of thy womb, Jesus. Holy Mary, Mother of God, pray for us sinners, now and at the hour of our death. Amen.

For an increase in the virtue of hope...I humbly pray:

(1) Hail Mary
Hail Mary, full of grace. The Lord is with thee. Blessed art thou amongst women, and blessed is the fruit of thy womb, Jesus. Holy Mary, Mother of God, pray for us sinners, now and at the hour of our death. Amen.

For an increase in the virtue of charity...I humbly pray:

(1) Hail Mary
Hail Mary, full of grace. The Lord is with thee. Blessed art thou amongst women, and blessed is the fruit of thy womb, Jesus. Holy Mary, Mother of God, pray for us sinners, now and at the hour of our death. Amen.

(1) Glory Be
Glory be to the Father, and to the Son, and to the Holy Spirit, as it was in the beginning, is now, and ever shall be, world without end. Amen.

(1) Oh my Jesus
Oh my Jesus, forgive us our sins, save us from the fires of hell and lead all souls into heaven, especially those in most need of thy mercy. Amen.

THE FIRST JOYFUL MYSTERY

THE ANNUNCIATION

Sweet Mother Mary, meditating on the Mystery of the Annunciation, which we read about in Luke 1:26-38 and John 1:14. When the angel Gabriel appeared to thee with the tidings that thou wert to become the Mother of God, greeting thee with that sublime salutation, "Hail, full of grace! the Lord is with thee!" and thou didst humbly submit thyself to the will of the Father, responding: "Behold the handmaid of the Lord. Be it done unto me according to thy word."

Meditating on the Mystery of The Annunciation and praying for an increase in the virtue of humility...I humbly pray

(1) Our Father

Our Father, Who art in Heaven, hallowed be Thy name; Thy kingdom come; Thy will be done on Earth as it is in Heaven. Give us this day our daily bread; and forgive us our trespasses as we forgive those who trespass against us; and lead us not into temptation, but deliver us from evil. Amen.

(10) Hail Mary

Hail Mary, full of grace. The Lord is with thee. Blessed art thou amongst women, and blessed is the fruit of thy womb, Jesus. Holy Mary, Mother of God, pray for us sinners, now and at the hour of our death. Amen.

(1) Glory Be

Glory be to the Father, and to the Son, and to the Holy Spirit, as it was in the beginning, is now, and ever shall be, world without end. Amen.

(1) Oh my Jesus

Oh my Jesus, forgive us our sins, save us from the fires of hell and lead all souls into heaven, especially those in most need of thy mercy. Amen.

I bind these snow-white roses with a petition for the virtue of

HUMILITY

and humbly lay this bouquet at thy feet.

THE SECOND JOYFUL MYSTERY

THE VISITATION

Sweet Mother Mary, meditating on the Mystery of the Visitation, which we read about in Luke 1:39-56. When, upon thy visit to thy holy cousin Elizabeth, she greeted thee with the prophetic utterance: "Blessed art thou among women, and blessed is the fruit of thy womb!" And thou didst answer with that canticle of canticles, the Magnificat.

Meditating on the Mystery of The Visitation, and praying for an increase in the virtue of charity, I humbly pray...

(1) Our Father

Our Father, Who art in Heaven, hallowed be Thy name; Thy kingdom come; Thy will be done on Earth as it is in Heaven. Give us this day our daily bread; and forgive us our trespasses as we forgive those who trespass against us; and lead us not into temptation, but deliver us from evil. Amen.

(10) Hail Mary

Hail Mary, full of grace. The Lord is with thee. Blessed art thou amongst women, and blessed is the fruit of thy womb, Jesus. Holy Mary, Mother of God, pray for us sinners, now and at the hour of our death. Amen.

(1) Glory Be

Glory be to the Father, and to the Son, and to the Holy Spirit, as it was in the beginning, is now, and ever shall be, world without end. Amen.

(1) Oh my Jesus

Oh my Jesus, forgive us our sins, save us from the fires of hell and lead all souls into heaven, especially those in most need of thy mercy. Amen.

I bind these snow-white roses with a petition for the virtue of

CHARITY

and humbly lay this bouquet at thy feet.

THE THIRD JOYFUL MYSTERY

THE NATIVITY

Sweet Mother Mary, meditating on the Mystery of the Nativity of Our Lord, which we read about in Matthew 1:18-25. When, thy time being completed, thou didst bring forth, O holy Virgin, the Redeemer of the world in a stable at Bethlehem. Whereupon choirs of angels filled the heavens with their exultant song of praise -- "Glory to God in the highest, and on Earth peace to men of good will"

Meditating on the Mystery of The Nativity, and praying for an increase in the virtue of detachment from the world, I humbly pray...

(1) Our Father

Our Father, Who art in Heaven, hallowed be Thy name; Thy kingdom come; Thy will be done on Earth as it is in Heaven. Give us this day our daily bread; and forgive us our trespasses as we forgive those who trespass against us; and lead us not into temptation, but deliver us from evil. Amen.

(10) Hail Mary

Hail Mary, full of grace. The Lord is with thee. Blessed art thou amongst women, and blessed is the fruit of thy womb, Jesus. Holy Mary, Mother of God, pray for us sinners, now and at the hour of our death. Amen.

(1) Glory Be

Glory be to the Father, and to the Son, and to the Holy Spirit, as it was in the beginning, is now, and ever shall be, world without end. Amen.

(1) Oh my Jesus

Oh my Jesus, forgive us our sins, save us from the fires of hell and lead all souls into heaven, especially those in most need of thy mercy. Amen.

I bind these snow-white roses with a petition for the virtue of

DETACHMENT FROM THE WORLD

and humbly lay this bouquet at thy feet.

THE FOURTH JOYFUL MYSTERY

THE PRESENTATION

Sweet Mother Mary, meditating on the Mystery of the Presentation, which we read about in Luke 2:22-39; when, in obedience to the Law of Moses, thou didst present thy Child in the Temple, where the holy prophet Simeon, taking the Child in his arms, offered thanks to God for sparing him to look upon his Savior and foretold thy sufferings by the words: "Thy soul also a sword shall pierce. . ."

Meditating of the Mystery of the Presentation of The Lord, and praying for an increase in the virtue of purity, I humbly pray...

(1) Our Father

Our Father, Who art in Heaven, hallowed be Thy name; Thy kingdom come; Thy will be done on Earth as it is in Heaven. Give us this day our daily bread; and forgive us our trespasses as we forgive those who trespass against us; and lead us not into temptation, but deliver us from evil. Amen.

(10) Hail Mary

Hail Mary, full of grace. The Lord is with thee. Blessed art thou amongst women, and blessed is the fruit of thy womb, Jesus. Holy Mary, Mother of God, pray for us sinners, now and at the hour of our death. Amen.

(1) Glory Be

Glory be to the Father, and to the Son, and to the Holy Spirit, as it was in the beginning, is now, and ever shall be, world without end. Amen.

(1) Oh my Jesus

Oh my Jesus, forgive us our sins, save us from the fires of hell and lead all souls into heaven, especially those in most need of thy mercy. Amen.

I bind these snow-white roses with a petition for the virtue of

PURITY

and humbly lay this bouquet at thy feet.

THE FIFTH JOYFUL MYSTERY

THE FINDING OF THE CHILD JESUS IN THE TEMPLE

Sweet Mother Mary, meditating on the Mystery of the Finding of the Child Jesus in the Temple, which we read about in Luke 2:41-51. When, having sought Him for three days, sorrowing, thy heart was gladdened upon finding Him in the Temple speaking to the doctors. And when, upon thy request, He obediently returned home with thee.

Meditating on the Mystery of The finding of the child Jesus in the Temple, and praying for an increase in the virtue of Obedience to the will of God, I humbly pray...

(1) Our Father

Our Father, Who art in Heaven, hallowed be Thy name; Thy kingdom come; Thy will be done on Earth as it is in Heaven. Give us this day our daily bread; and forgive us our trespasses as we forgive those who trespass against us; and lead us not into temptation, but deliver us from evil. Amen.

(10) Hail Mary

Hail Mary, full of grace. The Lord is with thee. Blessed art thou amongst women, and blessed is the fruit of thy womb, Jesus. Holy Mary, Mother of God, pray for us sinners, now and at the hour of our death. Amen.

(1) Glory Be

Glory be to the Father, and to the Son, and to the Holy Spirit, as it was in the beginning, is now, and ever shall be, world without end. Amen.

(1) Oh my Jesus

Oh my Jesus, forgive us our sins, save us from the fires of hell and lead all souls into heaven, especially those in most need of thy mercy. Amen.

I bind these snow-white roses with a petition for the virtue of

OBEDIENCE TO THE WILL OF GOD

and humbly lay this bouquet at thy feet.

SPIRITUAL COMMUNION

MY JESUS, really present in the most holy Sacrament of the Altar, since I cannot now receive Thee under the sacramental veil, I beseech Thee, with a heart full of love and longing, to come spiritually into my soul through the immaculate heart of Thy most holy Mother, and abide with me forever; Thou in me, and I in Thee, in time and in eternity, in Mary. Amen.

Hail Holy Queen

Hail, Holy Queen, Mother of mercy, our life, our sweetness and our hope. To thee do we cry, poor banished children of Eve: to thee do we send up our sighs, mourning and weeping in this valley of tears. Turn then, most gracious Advocate, thine eyes of mercy toward us, and after this our exile, show unto us the blessed fruit of thy womb, Jesus. O clement, O loving, O sweet Virgin Mary! Pray for us, O Holy Mother of God... that we may be made worthy of the promises of Christ. Amen

LET US PRAY

O God! Whose only-begotten Son, by His life, death, and resurrection, has purchased for us the reward of eternal life; grant, we beseech Thee, that, meditating upon these mysteries of the Most Holy Rosary of the Blessed Virgin Mary, we may imitate what they contain and obtain what they promise. Through the same Christ our Lord. Amen.

May the divine assistance remain always with us. Amen. And may the souls of the faithful departed, through the mercy *of* God, rest in peace. Amen. Holy Virgin, with thy loving Child, thy blessing give to us this day *(night)*.

Memorare

Remember, O most gracious Virgin Mary, that never was it known that anyone who fled to thy protection, implored thy help or sought thy intercession, was left unaided. Inspired by this confidence, We fly unto thee, O Virgin of virgins my Mother; to thee do we come, before thee we stand, sinful and sorrowful; O Mother of the Word Incarnate,

despise not our petitions, but in thy mercy hear and answer them. Amen.

Saint Michael Prayer
Saint Michael, the Archangel, defend us in battle. Be our protection against the wickedness and snares of the devil. May God rebuke him, we humbly pray; and do thou, O Prince of the heavenly host, by the power of God cast into hell Satan and all the evil spirits who prowl throughout the world seeking the ruin of souls. Amen.

Sign of the Cross
In the name of the Father, and the Son, and the Holy Spirit, Amen.

What Page to Turn to Next:

If today is a Monday then turn to page 39 to prepare for the Sorrowful Mysteries tomorrow on Tuesday.

If today is a Saturday then turn to page 5 to prepare for the Glorious Mysteries tomorrow on Sunday.

TUESDAY & FRIDAY

The Sorrowful Mysteries

HOW TO PRAY THE ROSARY

The image on the next page, and the steps below will show you how to pray the Rosary and also display the steps on a set of rosary beads*. These steps are just an overview. They are presented in order, and in more detail for each of the days that follow in the Rosary. The individual prayers for are also written out for you in the pages that follow for the Rosary.

Note: The image of the rosary that shows these steps on rosary beads were used with permission from The Rosary Foundation at www.erosary.com

HOW TO PRAY THE ROSARY STEPS

1. Make the Sign of The Cross and Say The Apostle's Creed.
2. Say one Our Father Prayer.
3. Say three Hail Mary Prayers.
4. Say one Glory Be To The Father Prayer.
5. Say one Fatima Prayer.
6. Announce the First Mystery and Say one Our Father prayer.
7. Say ten consecutive Hail Mary prayers; meditate on the first mystery as you are praying.
8. Say one Glory Be To The Father Prayer.
9. Say one Fatima Prayer.
10. Repeat steps 7, 8, and 9 for the second, third, fourth and fifth mysteries of The Rosary.
11. Say one Hail Holy Queen Prayer.
12. Make The Sign of The Cross

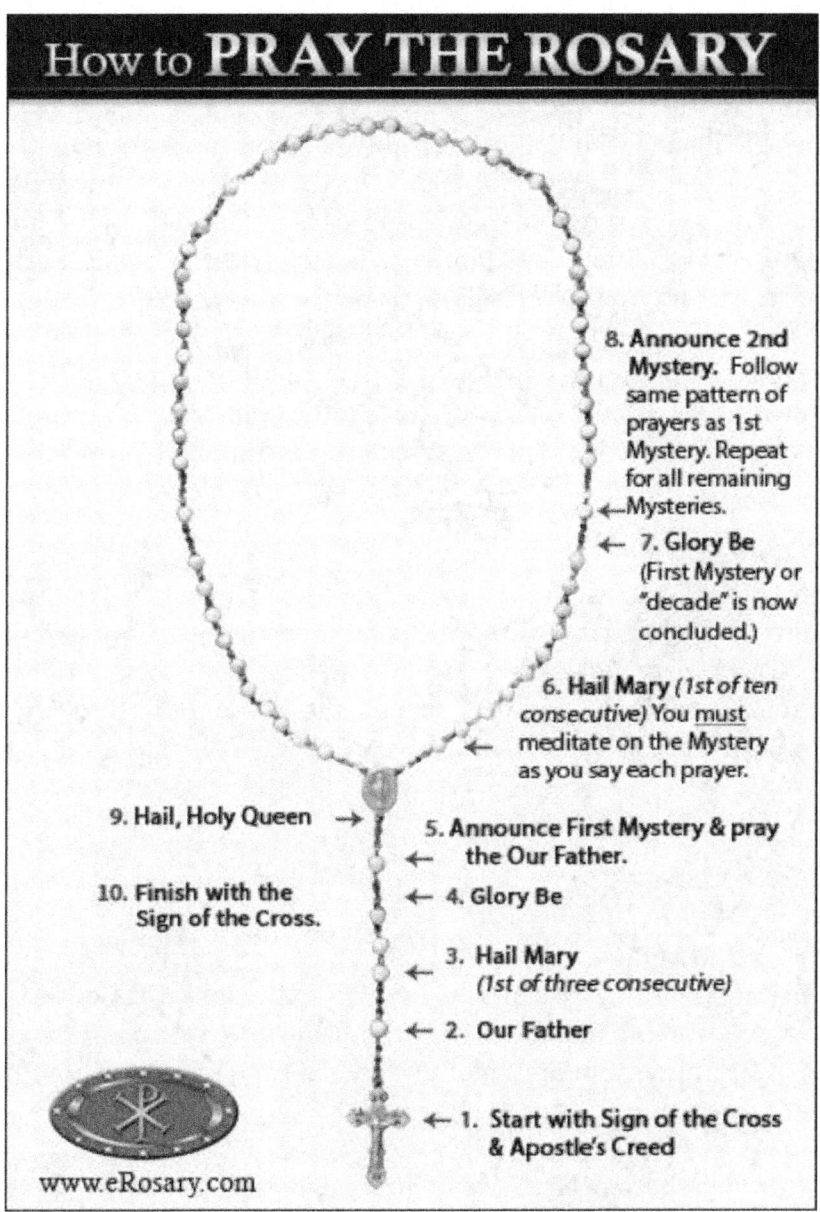

Image Courtesy of Dan Rudden at The Rosary Foundation.

THE MOST HOLY ROSARY

The Apostle's Creed
I believe in God, the Father Almighty, Creator of Heaven and Earth; and in Jesus Christ, His only Son, Our Lord, Who was conceived by the Holy Spirit, born of the Virgin Mary, suffered under Pontius Pilate, was crucified, died, and was buried. He descended into Hell. The third day He arose again from the dead; He ascended into Heaven, sitteth at the right hand of God, the Father Almighty; from thence He shall come to judge the living and the dead. I believe in the Holy Spirit, the holy Catholic Church, the communion of saints, the forgiveness of sins, the resurrection of the body, and the life everlasting. Amen.

(1) Our Father
Our Father, Who art in Heaven, hallowed be Thy name; Thy kingdom come; Thy will be done on Earth as it is in Heaven. Give us this day our daily bread; and forgive us our trespasses as we forgive those who trespass against us; and lead us not into temptation, but deliver us from evil. Amen.

The 3 Hail Mary beads

For an increase in the virtue of faith...I humbly pray:

(1) Hail Mary
Hail Mary, full of grace. The Lord is with thee. Blessed art thou amongst women, and blessed is the fruit of thy womb, Jesus. Holy Mary, Mother of God, pray for us sinners, now and at the hour of our death. Amen.

For an increase in the virtue of hope...I humbly pray:

(1) Hail Mary
Hail Mary, full of grace. The Lord is with thee. Blessed art thou amongst women, and blessed is the fruit of thy womb, Jesus. Holy Mary, Mother of God, pray for us sinners, now and at the hour of our death. Amen.

For an increase in the virtue of charity...I humbly pray:

(1) Hail Mary
Hail Mary, full of grace. The Lord is with thee. Blessed art thou amongst women, and blessed is the fruit of thy womb, Jesus. Holy Mary, Mother of God, pray for us sinners, now and at the hour of our death. Amen.

(1) Glory Be
Glory be to the Father, and to the Son, and to the Holy Spirit, as it was in the beginning, is now, and ever shall be, world without end. Amen.

(1) Oh my Jesus
Oh my Jesus, forgive us our sins, save us from the fires of hell and lead all souls into heaven, especially those in most need of thy mercy. Amen.

THE FIRST SORROWFUL MYSTERY

THE AGONY IN THE GARDEN

O most sorrowful Mother Mary, meditating on the Mystery of the Agony of Our Lord in the Garden, which we read about in Matthew 26:36-46, Mark 14:32-42, and Luke 22:39-46. When, in the grotto of the Garden of Olives, Jesus saw the sins of the world unfolded before Him by Satan, who sought to dissuade Him from the sacrifice He was about to make. When, His soul shrinking from the sight, and His precious blood flowing from every pore at the vision of the torture and death He was to undergo: thy own sufferings, dear Mother, the future sufferings of His Church, and His own sufferings in the Blessed Sacrament, He cried in anguish, "Abba! Father! if it be possible, let this chalice pass from Me!" But, immediately resigning Himself to His Father's will, He prayed, "Not as I will, but as Thou wilt!"

Meditating on the Mystery of The Agony in the Garden, and praying for an increase in the virtue of Resignation to the Will of God, I humbly pray...

(1) Our Father

Our Father, Who art in Heaven, hallowed be Thy name; Thy kingdom come; Thy will be done on Earth as it is in Heaven. Give us this day our daily bread; and forgive us our trespasses as we forgive those who trespass against us; and lead us not into temptation, but deliver us from evil. Amen.

(10) Hail Mary

Hail Mary, full of grace. The Lord is with thee. Blessed art thou amongst women, and blessed is the fruit of thy womb, Jesus. Holy Mary, Mother of God, pray for us sinners, now and at the hour of our death. Amen.

(1) Glory Be

Glory be to the Father, and to the Son, and to the Holy Spirit, as it was in the beginning, is now, and ever shall be, world without end. Amen.

(1) Oh my Jesus:

Oh my Jesus, forgive us our sins, save us from the fires of hell and lead all souls into heaven, especially those in most need of thy mercy. Amen.

I bind these blood red roses with a petition for the virtue of

RESIGNATION TO THE WILL OF GOD

and humbly lay this bouquet at your feet.

THE SECOND SORROWFUL MYSTERY

THE SCOURGING AT THE PILLAR

O most sorrowful Mother Mary, meditating on the Mystery of the Scourging of Our Lord, which we read about in Matthew 27:26, Mark 15:15, Luke 23:16-22, and John 19:1. When, at Pilate's command, thy divine Son, stripped of His garments and bound to a pillar, was lacerated from head to foot with cruel scourges and His flesh torn away until His mortified body could bear no more.

Meditating on the Mystery of the Scourging at the Pillar and praying for an increase in the virtue of Mortification, I humbly pray...

(1) Our Father

Our Father, Who art in Heaven, hallowed be Thy name; Thy kingdom come; Thy will be done on Earth as it is in Heaven. Give us this day our daily bread; and forgive us our trespasses as we forgive those who trespass against us; and lead us not into temptation, but deliver us from evil. Amen.

(10) Hail Mary

Hail Mary, full of grace. The Lord is with thee. Blessed art thou amongst women, and blessed is the fruit of thy womb, Jesus. Holy Mary, Mother of God, pray for us sinners, now and at the hour of our death. Amen.

(1) Glory Be

Glory be to the Father, and to the Son, and to the Holy Spirit, as it was in the beginning, is now, and ever shall be, world without end. Amen.

(1) Oh my Jesus:

Oh my Jesus, forgive us our sins, save us from the fires of hell and lead all souls into heaven, especially those in most need of thy mercy. Amen.

I bind these blood red roses with a petition for the virtue of

MORTIFICATION

and humbly lay this bouquet at your feet.

THE THIRD SORROWFUL MYSTERY

THE CROWNING WITH THORNS

O most sorrowful Mother Mary, meditating, on the Mystery of the Crowning of Our Lord with thorns, which we read about in Matthew 27:29-30, Mark 15:16-20, and John 19: 2-3. When, the soldiers, binding about His head a crown of sharp thorns, showered blows upon it, driving the thorns deeply into His head. When they then, in mock adoration, knelt before Him, crying, "Hail, King of the Jews!'

Meditating on the Mystery of The Crowning of Thorns and praying for an increase in the virtue of humility, I humbly pray...

(1) Our Father

Our Father, Who art in Heaven, hallowed be Thy name; Thy kingdom come; Thy will be done on Earth as it is in Heaven. Give us this day our daily bread; and forgive us our trespasses as we forgive those who trespass against us; and lead us not into temptation, but deliver us from evil. Amen.

(10) Hail Mary

Hail Mary, full of grace. The Lord is with thee. Blessed art thou amongst women, and blessed is the fruit of thy womb, Jesus. Holy Mary, Mother of God, pray for us sinners, now and at the hour of our death. Amen.

(1) Glory Be

Glory be to the Father, and to the Son, and to the Holy Spirit, as it was in the beginning, is now, and ever shall be, world without end. Amen.

(1) Oh my Jesus:

Oh my Jesus, forgive us our sins, save us from the fires of hell and lead all souls into heaven, especially those in most need of thy mercy. Amen.

I bind these blood red roses with a petition for the virtue of

HUMILITY

and humbly lay this bouquet at your feet.

THE FOURTH SORROWFUL MYSTERY

THE CARRYING OF THE CROSS

O most sorrowful Mother Mary, meditating on the Mystery of the Carrying of the Cross, which we read about in Luke 23: 26-32, Matthew 27:31-32, Mark 15:21, and John 19:17. When, with the heavy wood of the cross upon His shoulders, thy divine Son was dragged, weak and suffering, yet patient, through the streets amidst the revilements of the people to Calvary, falling often, but urged along by the cruel blows of His executioners.

Meditating on the Mystery of the Carrying of The Cross, and praying for an increase in the virtue of Patience in Adversity, I humbly pray...

(1) Our Father

Our Father, Who art in Heaven, hallowed be Thy name; Thy kingdom come; Thy will be done on Earth as it is in Heaven. Give us this day our daily bread; and forgive us our trespasses as we forgive those who trespass against us; and lead us not into temptation, but deliver us from evil. Amen.

(10) Hail Mary

Hail Mary, full of grace. The Lord is with thee. Blessed art thou amongst women, and blessed is the fruit of thy womb, Jesus. Holy Mary, Mother of God, pray for us sinners, now and at the hour of our death. Amen.

(1) Glory Be

Glory be to the Father, and to the Son, and to the Holy Spirit, as it was in the beginning, is now, and ever shall be, world without end. Amen.

(1) Oh my Jesus:

Oh my Jesus, forgive us our sins, save us from the fires of hell and lead all souls into heaven, especially those in most need of thy mercy. Amen.

I bind these blood red roses with a petition for the virtue of

PATIENCE IN ADVERSITY

and humbly lay this bouquet at your feet.

THE FIFTH SORROWFUL MYSTERY

THE CRUCIFIXION

O most Sorrowful Mother Mary, meditating on the Mystery of the Crucifixion, which we read about in Luke 23: 33-49; Matthew 27: 33-54; Mark 15: 22-39; and John 19: 17-37; when having been stripped of His garments, thy divine Son was nailed to the cross, upon which He died after three hours of indescribable agony, during which time He begged from His Father forgiveness for His enemies.

Meditating on the Mystery of the Crucifixion, and praying for an increase in the virtue of Love of our Enemies, I humbly pray...

(1) Our Father

Our Father, Who art in Heaven, hallowed be Thy name; Thy kingdom come; Thy will be done on Earth as it is in Heaven. Give us this day our daily bread; and forgive us our trespasses as we forgive those who trespass against us; and lead us not into temptation, but deliver us from evil. Amen.

(10) Hail Mary

Hail Mary, full of grace. The Lord is with thee. Blessed art thou amongst women, and blessed is the fruit of thy womb, Jesus. Holy Mary, Mother of God, pray for us sinners, now and at the hour of our death. Amen.

(1) Glory Be

Glory be to the Father, and to the Son, and to the Holy Spirit, as it was in the beginning, is now, and ever shall be, world without end. Amen.

(1) Oh my Jesus:

Oh my Jesus, forgive us our sins, save us from the fires of hell and lead all souls into heaven, especially those in most need of thy mercy. Amen.

I bind these blood red roses with a petition for the virtue of

LOVE OF OUR ENEMIES

and humbly lay this bouquet at your feet.

SPIRITUAL COMMUNION

MY JESUS, really present in the most holy Sacrament of the Altar, since I cannot now receive Thee under the sacramental veil, I beseech Thee, with a heart full of love and longing, to come spiritually into my soul through the immaculate heart of Thy most holy Mother, and abide with me forever; Thou in me, and I in Thee, in time and in eternity, in Mary. Amen.

Hail Holy Queen

Hail, Holy Queen, Mother of mercy, our life, our sweetness and our hope. To thee do we cry, poor banished children of Eve: to thee do we send up our sighs, mourning and weeping in this valley of tears. Turn then, most gracious Advocate, thine eyes of mercy toward us, and after this our exile, show unto us the blessed fruit of thy womb, Jesus. O clement, O loving, O sweet Virgin Mary! Pray for us, O Holy Mother of God... that we may be made worthy of the promises of Christ. Amen

LET US PRAY

O God! Whose only-begotten Son, by His life, death, and resurrection, has purchased for us the reward of eternal life; grant, we beseech Thee, that, meditating upon these mysteries of the Most Holy Rosary of the Blessed Virgin Mary, we may imitate what they contain and obtain what they promise. Through the same Christ our Lord. Amen.

May the divine assistance remain always with us. Amen. And may the souls of the faithful departed, through the mercy of God, rest in peace. Amen. Holy Virgin, with thy loving Child, thy blessing give to us this day *(night)*.

Memorare

Remember, O most gracious Virgin Mary, that never was it known that anyone who fled to thy protection, implored thy help or sought thy intercession, was left unaided. Inspired by this confidence, We fly unto thee, O Virgin of virgins my Mother; to thee do we come, before thee we stand, sinful and sorrowful; O Mother of the Word Incarnate,

despise not our petitions, but in thy mercy hear and answer them. Amen.

Saint Michael Prayer
Saint Michael, the Archangel, defend us in battle. Be our protection against the wickedness and snares of the devil. May God rebuke him, we humbly pray; and do thou, O Prince of the heavenly host, by the power of God cast into hell Satan and all the evil spirits who prowl throughout the world seeking the ruin of souls. Amen.

Sign of the Cross
In the name of the Father, and the Son, and the Holy Spirit, Amen.

What Page to Turn to Next:

If today is a Tuesday then turn to page 5 to prepare for the Glorious Mysteries tomorrow on Wednesday.

If today is a Friday then turn to page 22 to prepare for the Joyful Mysteries tomorrow on Saturday.

THURSDAY

The Luminous Mysteries

HOW TO PRAY THE ROSARY

The image on the next page, and the steps below will show you how to pray the Rosary and also display the steps on a set of rosary beads*. These steps are just an overview. They are presented in order, and in more detail for each of the days that follow in the Rosary. The individual prayers for are also written out for you in the pages that follow for the Rosary.

Note: The image of the rosary that shows these steps on rosary beads were used with permission from The Rosary Foundation at www.erosary.com

HOW TO PRAY THE ROSARY STEPS

1. Make the Sign of The Cross and Say The Apostle's Creed.
2. Say one Our Father Prayer.
3. Say three Hail Mary Prayers.
4. Say one Glory Be To The Father Prayer.
5. Say one Fatima Prayer.
6. Announce the First Mystery and Say one Our Father prayer.
7. Say ten consecutive Hail Mary prayers; meditate on the first mystery as you are praying.
8. Say one Glory Be To The Father Prayer.
9. Say one Fatima Prayer.
10. Repeat steps 7, 8, and 9 for the second, third, fourth and fifth mysteries of The Rosary.
11. Say one Hail Holy Queen Prayer.
12. Make The Sign of The Cross

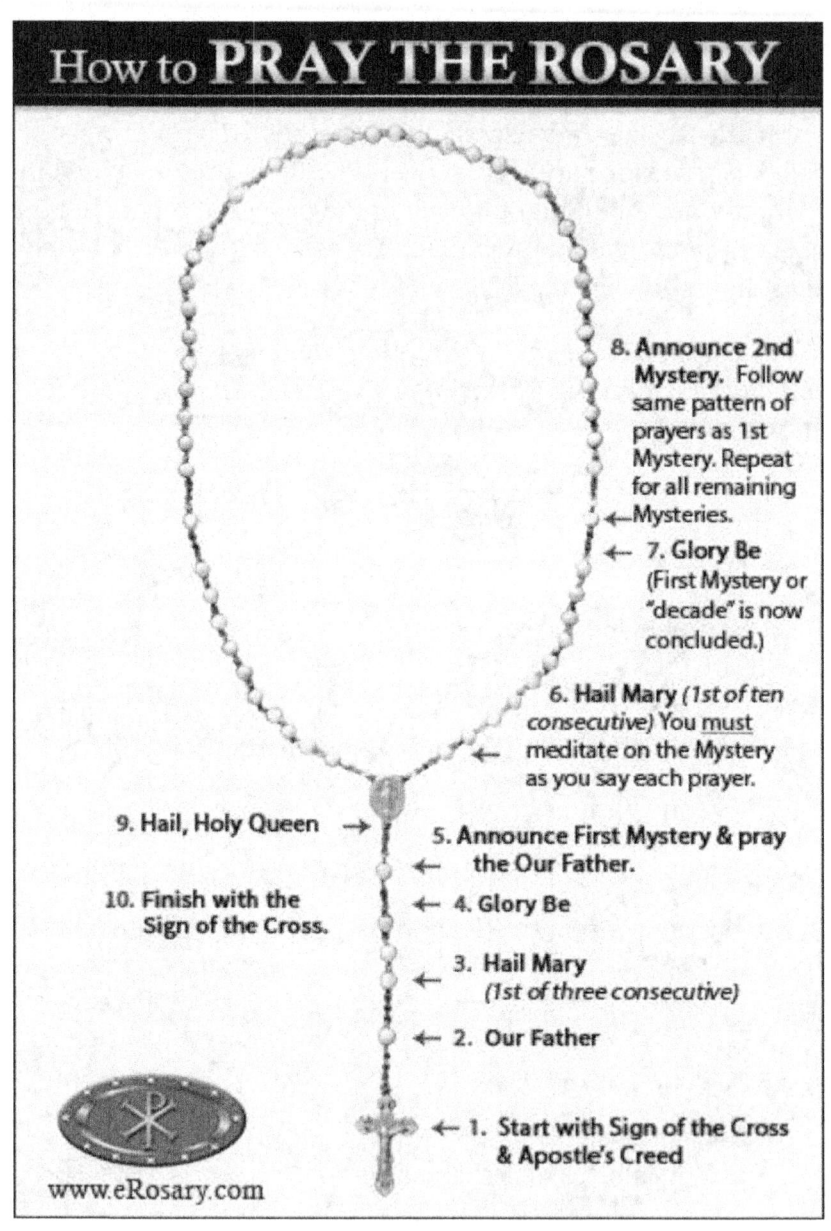

Image Courtesy of Dan Rudden at The Rosary Foundation.

THE MOST HOLY ROSARY

The Apostle's Creed
I believe in God, the Father Almighty, Creator of Heaven and Earth; and in Jesus Christ, His only Son, Our Lord, Who was conceived by the Holy Spirit, born of the Virgin Mary, suffered under Pontius Pilate, was crucified, died, and was buried. He descended into Hell. The third day He arose again from the dead; He ascended into Heaven, sitteth at the right hand of God, the Father Almighty; from thence He shall come to judge the living and the dead. I believe in the Holy Spirit, the holy Catholic Church, the communion of saints, the forgiveness of sins, the resurrection of the body, and the life everlasting. Amen.

(1) Our Father
Our Father, Who art in Heaven, hallowed be Thy name; Thy kingdom come; Thy will be done on Earth as it is in Heaven. Give us this day our daily bread; and forgive us our trespasses as we forgive those who trespass against us; and lead us not into temptation, but deliver us from evil. Amen.

The 3 Hail Mary beads

For an increase in the virtue of faith...I humbly pray:

(1) Hail Mary
Hail Mary, full of grace. The Lord is with thee. Blessed art thou amongst women, and blessed is the fruit of thy womb, Jesus. Holy Mary, Mother of God, pray for us sinners, now and at the hour of our death. Amen.

For an increase in the virtue of hope...I humbly pray:

(1) Hail Mary
Hail Mary, full of grace. The Lord is with thee. Blessed art thou amongst women, and blessed is the fruit of thy womb, Jesus. Holy Mary, Mother of God, pray for us sinners, now and at the hour of our death. Amen.

For an increase in the virtue of charity...I humbly pray:

(1) Hail Mary
Hail Mary, full of grace. The Lord is with thee. Blessed art thou amongst women, and blessed is the fruit of thy womb, Jesus. Holy Mary, Mother of God, pray for us sinners, now and at the hour of our death. Amen.

(1) Glory Be
Glory be to the Father, and to the Son, and to the Holy Spirit, as it was in the beginning, is now, and ever shall be, world without end. Amen.

(1) Oh my Jesus
Oh my Jesus, forgive us our sins, save us from the fires of hell and lead all souls into heaven, especially those in most need of thy mercy. Amen.

THE FIRST MYSTERY OF LIGHT

THE BAPTISM OF JESUS IN THE JORDAN RIVER

O Courageous Mother Mary, meditating on the Mystery of the Baptism of Jesus in the Jordan River which we read about in Matthew 3:11-17; Mark 1:9-11; Luke 3:15-22 and John 1:26-34. When your son, as an example to all, insisted on being baptized by his cousin John and the sky opened and the Holy Spirit came down to him like a dove and a voice from heaven said, "You are my own dear Son in whom I am well pleased."

Meditating on the Baptism of Jesus in the Jordan River and praying for an increase in the virtue of Openness To The Holy Spirit, I humbly pray...

(1) Our Father

Our Father, Who art in Heaven, hallowed be Thy name; Thy kingdom come; Thy will be done on Earth as it is in Heaven. Give us this day our daily bread; and forgive us our trespasses as we forgive those who trespass against us; and lead us not into temptation, but deliver us from evil. Amen.

(10) Hail Mary

Hail Mary, full of grace. The Lord is with thee. Blessed art thou amongst women, and blessed is the fruit of thy womb, Jesus. Holy Mary, Mother of God, pray for us sinners, now and at the hour of our death. Amen.

(1) Glory Be

Glory be to the Father, and to the Son, and to the Holy Spirit, as it was in the beginning, is now, and ever shall be, world without end. Amen.

Oh my Jesus:

Oh my Jesus, forgive us our sins, save us from the fires of hell and lead all souls into heaven, especially those in most need of thy mercy. Amen.

I bind these bright yellow roses with a petition for the virtue of

OPENNESS TO THE HOLY SPIRIT

and humbly lay this bouquet at thy feet.

THE SECOND MYSTERY OF LIGHT

THE WEDDING OF CANA...THE FIRST MIRACLE OF JESUS...

O Courageous Mother Mary, meditating on the Mystery of the First Miracle of Jesus at the Wedding Feast at Cana, the story that we read about in John 2:1-12, when at your urging, your son performed the first of his many miracles by helping a couple celebrate their marriage by changing water into wine of such quality that the chief steward upbraided the host by saying, "Usually people serve the best wine first and save the cheaper wine for last, but you have saved the choice wine for last."

Meditating on the Mystery of The Wedding Feast at Cana, and praying for an increase in the virtue of To Jesus Through Mary, I humbly pray...

(1) Our Father

Our Father, Who art in Heaven, hallowed be Thy name; Thy kingdom come; Thy will be done on Earth as it is in Heaven. Give us this day our daily bread; and forgive us our trespasses as we forgive those who trespass against us; and lead us not into temptation, but deliver us from evil. Amen.

(10) Hail Mary

Hail Mary, full of grace. The Lord is with thee. Blessed art thou amongst women, and blessed is the fruit of thy womb, Jesus. Holy Mary, Mother of God, pray for us sinners, now and at the hour of our death. Amen.

(1) Glory Be

Glory be to the Father, and to the Son, and to the Holy Spirit, as it was in the beginning, is now, and ever shall be, world without end. Amen.

(1) Oh my Jesus:

Oh my Jesus, forgive us our sins, save us from the fires of hell and lead all souls into heaven, especially those in most need of thy mercy. Amen.

I bind these bright yellow roses with a petition for the virtue of

TO JESUS THROUGH MARY

and humbly lay this bouquet at your feet.

THE THIRD MYSTERY OF LIGHT

THE PROCLAMATION OF THE KINGDOM OF GOD

O courageous Mother Mary, meditating on the Mystery of the Proclamation of the Kingdom of God, the story that we read about in Mark 1:14-15, Matthew 5:1-16, Matthew 6:33, and also Matthew 7:21, when your son revealed that the reign of God has already begun "within us" and we are called to conversion and forgiveness, praying "Your Kingdom come, your will be done, on Earth as it is in heaven."

Meditating on the Mystery of the Proclamation of the Kingdom of God, and praying for an increase in the virtue of Repentance and Trust in God, I humbly pray...

(1) Our Father

Our Father, Who art in Heaven, hallowed be Thy name; Thy kingdom come; Thy will be done on Earth as it is in Heaven. Give us this day our daily bread; and forgive us our trespasses as we forgive those who trespass against us; and lead us not into temptation, but deliver us from evil. Amen.

(10) Hail Mary

Hail Mary, full of grace. The Lord is with thee. Blessed art thou amongst women, and blessed is the fruit of thy womb, Jesus. Holy Mary, Mother of God, pray for us sinners, now and at the hour of our death. Amen.

(1) Glory Be

Glory be to the Father, and to the Son, and to the Holy Spirit, as it was in the beginning, is now, and ever shall be, world without end. Amen.

(1) Oh my Jesus:

Oh my Jesus, forgive us our sins, save us from the fires of hell and lead all souls into heaven, especially those in most need of thy mercy. Amen.

I bind these bright yellow roses with a petition for the virtue of

REPENTANCE AND TRUST IN GOD

and humbly lay this bouquet at your feet.

THE FOURTH MYSTERY OF LIGHT

THE TRANSFIGURATION

O courageous Mother Mary, meditating on the Mystery of the Transfiguration, the story that we read about in Matthew 17:1-8, Mark 9:2-10, and Luke 9:28-36, when your son revealed his glory to his three disciples, appearing on a mountain with Moses and Elijah, his face shining like the sun and a voice from heaven proclaiming, "This is my beloved Son...Listen to him."

Meditating on the Mystery of The Transfiguration, and praying for an increase in the virtue of Desire for Holiness, I humbly pray...

(1) Our Father

Our Father, Who art in Heaven, hallowed be Thy name; Thy kingdom come; Thy will be done on Earth as it is in Heaven. Give us this day our daily bread; and forgive us our trespasses as we forgive those who trespass against us; and lead us not into temptation, but deliver us from evil. Amen.

(10) Hail Mary

Hail Mary, full of grace. The Lord is with thee. Blessed art thou amongst women, and blessed is the fruit of thy womb, Jesus. Holy Mary, Mother of God, pray for us sinners, now and at the hour of our death. Amen.

(1) Glory Be

Glory be to the Father, and to the Son, and to the Holy Spirit, as it was in the beginning, is now, and ever shall be, world without end. Amen.

(1) Oh my Jesus:

Oh my Jesus, forgive us our sins, save us from the fires of hell and lead all souls into heaven, especially those in most need of thy mercy. Amen.

I bind these bright yellow roses with a petition for the virtue of

DESIRE FOR HOLINESS

and humbly lay this bouquet at your feet.

THE FIFTH MYSTERY OF LIGHT

THE INSTITUTION OF THE EUCHARIST

O courageous Mother Mary, meditating on the Mystery of the Institution of the Sacrament of the Eucharist, the lesson we are taught in Matthew 26:26-28, Mark 14:22-25, Luke 22:14-20, and John 6:33-59, when on the day before he died, your son celebrated the Passover with his disciples and took bread and gave it to them saying, "Take and eat; this is my body." And when dinner was finished he took a cup of wine and shared it with them saying, "Take and drink; this is my blood, which will be given up for you; do this in memory of me."

Meditating on the Institution of The Eucharist and praying for an increase in the virtue of Adoration of The Eucharist, I humbly pray...

(1) Our Father

Our Father, Who art in Heaven, hallowed be Thy name; Thy kingdom come; Thy will be done on Earth as it is in Heaven. Give us this day our daily bread; and forgive us our trespasses as we forgive those who trespass against us; and lead us not into temptation, but deliver us from evil. Amen.

(10) Hail Mary

Hail Mary, full of grace. The Lord is with thee. Blessed art thou amongst women, and blessed is the fruit of thy womb, Jesus. Holy Mary, Mother of God, pray for us sinners, now and at the hour of our death. Amen.

(1) Glory Be

Glory be to the Father, and to the Son, and to the Holy Spirit, as it was in the beginning, is now, and ever shall be, world without end. Amen.

(1) Oh my Jesus:

Oh my Jesus, forgive us our sins, save us from the fires of hell and lead all souls into heaven, especially those in most need of thy mercy. Amen.

I bind these bright yellow roses with a petition for the virtue of

ADORATION OF THE EUCHARIST

and humbly lay this bouquet at your feet.

SPIRITUAL COMMUNION

MY JESUS, really present in the most holy Sacrament of the Altar, since I cannot now receive Thee under the sacramental veil, I beseech Thee, with a heart full of love and longing, to come spiritually into my soul through the immaculate heart of Thy most holy Mother, and abide with me forever; Thou in me, and I in Thee, in time and in eternity, in Mary. Amen.

Hail Holy Queen

Hail, Holy Queen, Mother of mercy, our life, our sweetness and our hope. To thee do we cry, poor banished children of Eve: to thee do we send up our sighs, mourning and weeping in this valley of tears. Turn then, most gracious Advocate, thine eyes of mercy toward us, and after this our exile, show unto us the blessed fruit of thy womb, Jesus. O clement, O loving, O sweet Virgin Mary! Pray for us, O Holy Mother of God... that we may be made worthy of the promises of Christ. Amen

LET US PRAY

O God! Whose only-begotten Son, by His life, death, and resurrection, has purchased for us the reward of eternal life; grant, we beseech Thee, that, meditating upon these mysteries of the Most Holy Rosary of the Blessed Virgin Mary, we may imitate what they contain and obtain what they promise. Through the same Christ our Lord. Amen.

May the divine assistance remain always with us. Amen. And may the souls of the faithful departed, through the mercy *of* God, rest in peace. Amen. Holy Virgin, with thy loving Child, thy blessing give to us this day *(night)*.

Memorare

Remember, O most gracious Virgin Mary, that never was it known that anyone who fled to thy protection, implored thy help or sought thy intercession, was left unaided. Inspired by this confidence, We fly unto thee, O Virgin of virgins my Mother; to thee do we come, before thee we stand, sinful and sorrowful; O Mother of the Word Incarnate,

despise not our petitions, but in thy mercy hear and answer them. Amen.

Saint Michael Prayer
Saint Michael, the Archangel, defend us in battle. Be our protection against the wickedness and snares of the devil. May God rebuke him, we humbly pray; and do thou, O Prince of the heavenly host, by the power of God cast into hell Satan and all the evil spirits who prowl throughout the world seeking the ruin of souls. Amen.

Sign of the Cross
In the name of the Father, and the Son, and the Holy Spirit, Amen.

What Page to Turn to Next:

Turn to page 39 to prepare for the Sorrowful Mysteries tomorrow on Friday.

A ROSARY STORY FROM:

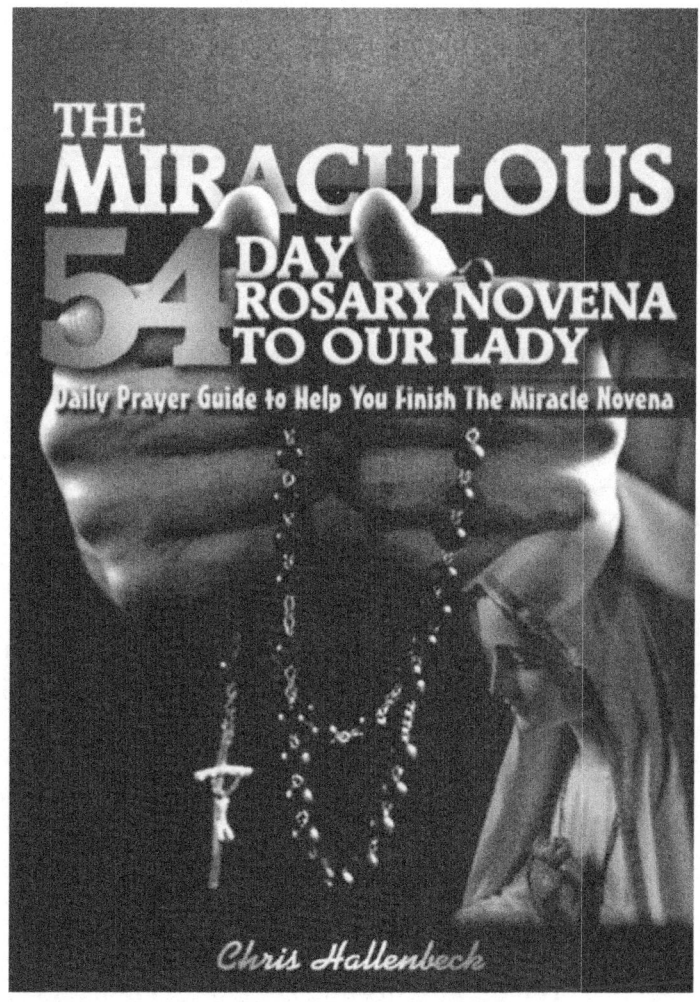

AVAILABLE ON GREATPOINTPUBLISHING.COM & AMAZON.COM

Note: In obedience to the decree of Pope Urban VIII (1623-1644) and of other Supreme Pontiffs, the author begs to state that, in regard to what is herein narrated, no higher authority is claimed than that which is due to all authentic human testimony.

AN INSPIRATIONAL ROSARY NOVENA STORY FROM GLOVERSVILLE, NY
By: Christopher Hallenbeck

There are special times in our lives when both you and I welcome Christ into our daily routines. Some of these routines could be small random acts of kindness or displays of charity that you try to practice habitually. Other times they could be special major events or milestones in your life. The events that are probably coming to your mind immediately are moments when you have received one of the seven sacraments; right now you might be recalling your first communion, receiving the sacrament of confirmation, going to confession during Lent and Advent seasons, or perhaps you're recalling the day that you were married to your wife or husband.

Sacraments are easy for you to remember because, according to the Catechism of the Catholic Church, "Seated at the right hand of the Father" and pouring out the Holy Spirit on his Body which is the Church… the sacraments are effective, valuable, and successful signs of grace, instituted by Christ and entrusted to the Church, by which divine life is dispensed to us…the sacraments strengthen faith and express it (CCC 1084, 1131,1133)[1].

The story that I'm about to share is not a recollection of a specific time that I received a particular sacrament. Instead it is the story of how I was introduced to the 54 Day Rosary Novena, and the blessings it has brought into my life, my family's life, and the blessings that it can bring into your life too. This story is five years in the making, and it wasn't until very recently that I first began to share this story. It was very private. I didn't want anyone else to know what I had discovered or what I was doing, and also there wasn't really much a story to share at the time.

Never in my wildest dreams did I ever imagine what would be brought into my life and my family's life five years later. All of this thanks be to God. The inspirational story about the 54 Day Rosary Novena to Our Lady in Gloversville, NY is a story about a special time that involves prayer, a sacrament, and strengthened faith. I hope you enjoy the read.

During Christmas in 2010, I was stumped on what to get my Grandma for a Christmas present. She was 91 at the time, and had been a devout Catholic all of her life. I usually would get her favorite candy, the chocolate and nut candy called Turtles, for her for Christmas. However, Grandma's teeth were becoming fragile and so my mom suggested that I think of something else to get her instead. So, I brainstormed in hopes of finding the perfect Christmas gift for my Grandma. Then the light bulb clicked! I thought of the perfect Christmas gift for her.

I'll get my Grandma a new set of Rosary beads. I'd never gotten her a set of Rosary beads before. She was always praying the Rosary, plus it was a thoughtful, creative, and meaningful gift. It was perfect! I searched online, and saw these beautiful blue Rosary beads that contained a picture of the Miraculous Medal on it, and I ordered a set. When they arrived, they were a lot nicer in person than the pictures I saw online, and my curiosity kicked in: what did each bead mean?

I learned how to say the Rosary in church school, but that had been a long time ago. So I ordered another set of the same Rosary beads for myself, and when they arrived I googled how to pray the Rosary. Next, I read everything that I could find on the Rosary. After doing so, there were three things that stood out to me at the time, and they have still stuck with me today.

The first thing that stood out to me was that I discovered the 54 Day Rosary Novena, also known as the Miraculous 54 Day Rosary Novena. If you're wondering why it is called the 54 Day Rosary Novena, here is the story behind why we say this Rosary for exactly 54 days, and how it was introduced to the Church:

Church history teaches us that in 1884 an apparition of Our Lady of Pompeii occurred inside the house of Commander Agrelli, an Italian military officer in Naples, Italy. For thirteen months, Fortuna

Agrelli, the daughter of the Commander, was very, very sick. She had been in great distress, experiencing dreadful sufferings, torturous cramps, and even near death. So serious was her illness that her case had been given-up as hopeless by the most celebrated physicians of the time.

In desperation, on February 16, 1884, the afflicted girl and her family began a novena of Rosaries. The Queen of the Holy Rosary favored her with an apparition on March 3rd. Mary, sitting upon a high throne, surrounded by luminous figures, held the divine Child on her lap, and in her hand a Rosary. The Virgin Mother and The Holy Infant were clad in gold embroidered garments. They were accompanied by St. Dominic and St. Catherine of Siena. The throne was profusely decorated with flowers; the beauty of Our Lady was marvelous. Mary looked upon the sufferer with maternal tenderness, and the patient Fortuna saluted Mary with the words:

> *"Queen of the Holy Rosary, be gracious to me; restore me to health! I have already prayed to thee in a novena, O Mary, but have not yet experienced thy aid. I am so anxious to be cured!"*

> *"Child,"* responded the Blessed Virgin, *"thou hast invoked me by various titles and hast always obtained favors from me. Now, since thou hast called me by that title so pleasing to me, 'Queen of the Holy Rosary,' I can no longer refuse the favor thou dost petition; for this name is most precious and dear to me. Make three novenas, and thou shalt obtain all."*

Once more the Queen of the Holy Rosary appeared to her and said,

> *"Whoever desires to obtain favors from me should make three novenas of the prayers of the Rosary, and three novenas in thanksgiving."*

Obedient to Our Lady's invitation, Fortuna and her family completed the six novenas whereupon the young girl Fortuna was restored to perfect health and her family was showered with many blessings.

Through her, Our Lady gave the world the miraculous devotion of the 54 day Rosary Novena.[2]

According to the Benedictine Convent of Perpetual Adoration in Clyde, Missouri, This miracle of the Rosary made a very deep impression on Pope Leo XIII, and greatly contributed to the fact that in so many circular letters he urged all Christians to love the Rosary and say it fervently.[2]

But, what's the reason behind you having to pray the Rosary for exactly 54 days?

The early Greeks had a penchant for abstract thinking, and they thought that numbers were the key to all knowledge. The first one who thought it all out was Pythagoras.[3]

Pythagoras was the first person to calculate the beautiful sounds of harmonies, and how notes sounded by chords make harmonic tones if the notes of the chords are all interrelated in simple numeric ratios. This is standard music theory knowledge that we still use today. Pythagoras also came up with Pythagorean Theorem. In case you don't remember it from grade school, this is the square of the hypotenuse of a right triangle is equal to the sum of the squares of the other two sides. Pythagoras also gave numbers religious meaning. Somehow he was able to discover that things weren't just measured by just a number, but somehow they were also caused by number, and Pythagoras also taught that you could see the mind of God at work by looking at the ways that numbers work.[3]

Many years after Pythagoras taught that numbers had a religious meaning, Saint Augustine lectured many times on the Gospel of John, Chapter 21, verses 1-14. During these lectures Saint Augustine would explain the significance, and importance of the symbolism of the 153 fish that were caught in the Sea of Tiberias when Jesus told the apostles to cast their nets to the right side of the boat. Catching 153 fish is a very specific number of fish. This is important because "He (Jesus) didn't say anything like that the previous time he directed their fishing (Lk 5:4); he had already told them that He intended for them to be fishers of men (Mt 4:19), and He described the Last Judgement in terms of taking the creatures to His right (Mt 25:31-46). So the fish in John 21 refer to people, and Saint Augustine said 'the number signifies thousands, and thousands…to be admitted into the Kingdom of Heaven.'"[3]

The reason he gives is because there are 10 Commandments that you have to follow to get into Heaven. However, no one keeps the Commandments by their own power. We need help, we all need the grace of God. The grace of God comes in terms of the sevenfold gifts of the Holy Spirit.

Saint Augustine teaches us that there is a need for the Spirit so that the Law can be fulfilled. So add 10 + 7. What do you get? …17.

According to Saint Augustine, however, you can't take this as a lump sum. It is necessary to account for every detail included in the seven gifts of the Holy Spirit and also the Ten Commandments and all of their implications, so when you add all of the numbers from 1 to 17, guess what number you get?…153!

This calculation according to Saint Augustine was why Saint John was so specific about the number of 153 fish caught; it lets you derive a general principle of salvation from a specific detail![4] This is important because it helps teach us why we pray the 54 Day Rosary Novena for 54 Days. Each number in the Bible has a traditional meaning dating from the time of Pythagoras, and contains a definite symbolic value today.

The number 3 stands for everything that is perfect. In Hebrew, Greek, and Christian thought, the third unit, unites the halves of 2. It reconciles any tension implied, bringing things to finish, to completion, to perfection! For example, the truth that the Holy Spirit "proceeds from the Father, and the Son," completes the Trinity. When you have three of anything, you have all that there is, or at least enough. That's why in Mass we say "Holy, Holy, Holy…" thrice Holy is as Holy as anything can be. It brings things to finish, to completion, to perfection![3]

During the apparition in 1884, when the Blessed Mother said to Fortuna:

> *"Whoever desires to obtain favors from me should make three novenas of the prayers of the Rosary, and three novenas in thanksgiving."*

A Novena is a Roman Catholic period of prayer lasting nine consecutive days.[4]

The number 9 is important because when you multiply 3 times 3 your answer is 9. Therefore, 9 is a symbol of perfection multiplied by perfection.[4]

When Our Lady first tells Fortuna to make 3 novenas of the prayers, she's telling her to pray for 9 days consecutively 3 times, therefore she's praying for 27 days in petition for her favor.

After praying for 27 days in petition, Our Lady then instructs Fortuna to say 3 more novenas in thanksgiving. Thus, she's telling Fortuna to pray in thanksgiving for 9 days consecutively 3 times, or 27 more days in thanksgiving.

When you add the 3 novenas in petition (27 days total), plus three more novenas in thanksgiving for your favor (27 more days), this is how you get and why you pray for exactly 54 days total during the Miraculous 54 Day Rosary Novena.

In 1926, author Charles V. Lacey wrote that the 54 day Rosary Novena is "a laborious Novena, but a Novena of Love. You who are sincere will not find it too difficult, if you really wish to obtain your request. Should you not obtain the favor you seek, be assured that the Rosary Queen, who knows what each one stands most in need of, has heard your prayer. You will not have prayed in vain. No prayer ever went unheard. And Our Blessed Lady has never been known to fail. Look upon each Hail Mary as a rare and beautiful rose which you lay at Mary's feet. These spiritual roses, bound in a wreath with Spiritual Communions, will be a most pleasing and acceptable gift to her, and will bring down upon you special graces. If you would reach the innermost recesses of her heart, lavishly bedeck your wreath with spiritual diamonds holy communions. Then her joy will be unbounded, and she will open wide the channel of her choicest graces to you."[2]

After reading about the 54 Day Rosary Novena, I decided that this was what I needed to help me learn the Rosary. The daily calendar would help keep me on track learning and saying the Rosary every day, and I also really liked the story of the miracle that occurred for the Agrelli family in 1884.

You see, in November 2010, my family was in need of a miracle at the time as well, and I felt that praying the 54 Day Rosary Novena was at the best way that I could help them. After all the miraculous Rosary Novena helped the Agrelli family in their time of need in 1884, and I wondered, could it help my family as well in 2010?

When I first read about the 54 day Rosary Novena, my brother and his wife and been trying to have a baby for about 18 months prior. I said to myself, "This is perfect! I'll say a 54 Day Rosary Novena for Mike and Diana to have a baby, and I'll get a Scapular so my prayers are as effective as can be."

On December 1, 2010, I began to say the 54 day Rosary Novena.

I also ordered myself a Brown Scapular around the same time. The power of the Rosary and Brown Scapular working together was the second thing I discovered that stood out to me when I was reading and relearning about the Rosary.

When my scapular arrived, inside there was a brief note explaining the history of the Brown Scapular and also recommending that first time wearers of the Brown Scapular should have their scapular blessed. I called the rectory at my parish the next day, and I talked to Father Don Czelusniak.

I explained to him that I just had gotten a new scapular and I asked him if he could bless it for me. Father Don said, "I can't do it this week, but Father Rendell can meet you." So I called Father Rendell Torres, and he told me to meet him at the rectory at 9am on January 6, 2011. It was the first Thursday of the month.

I remember this day specifically, because after Father Rendell blessed my scapular he told me that I should stop by the Church later to attend Adoration. They have Adoration of the Blessed Sacrament every Thursday, and that prayers were very powerful before the Blessed Sacrament.

That was all that I needed to hear.

At the time I'd never been to Adoration of the Blessed Sacrament, but when Father Rendell said that prayers before the Blessed Sacrament were very powerful, I knew right there that I needed to stop by after work to pray my daily rosary before the Blessed Sacrament.

Later that day, I did exactly that. After I got out of work, I went back to the Church of the Holy Spirit in Gloversville to visit Adoration of the Blessed Sacrament. I remember specifically that as I walked through the church, my newly blessed Scapular felt alive with the Holy Spirit as I walked in through the front doors. I kneeled down and prayed the Rosary before the Blessed Sacrament, continuing on with my 54 Day Rosary Novena.

In the following months I would try my best to make sure I'd say my daily Rosary on the first Thursday of the month in front of the Blessed Sacrament.

54 days later, I finished my first 54 day Rosary Novena. My brother and his wife were still not expecting. I thought I messed up somehow.

The next day I started to pray another 54 Day Rosary Novena, same format, visiting Adoration of the Blessed Sacrament every first Thursday of the month, and again praying for my brother and his wife to have a baby.

54 days later, I finished my second 54 Day Rosary Novena. And once again, my brother and his wife were still not expecting.

The next day, 109 days after I first started praying the Rosary, I began a third 54 day Rosary Novena, once again with the same format: visiting the Blessed Sacrament every first Thursday, and praying for my brother and his wife to have a baby.

54 days later, I finished my third 54 Day Rosary Novena. And once again, my brother and his wife were still not expecting.

After 162 days of praying the Rosary, I kind of got sick of praying the 54 Day Rosary Novena, and I needed a break. But what I didn't stop doing was visiting the Blessed Sacrament every first Thursday of the month.

In August of 2011, my Grandma was diagnosed with cancer. The week after her diagnosis, it happened to be the first Thursday of the month of August, so I visited Adoration of the Blessed Sacrament. I wasn't expecting a miracle, but I prayed that my grandmother would be in the least amount of pain as possible, and that she wouldn't have to suffer. The following week she passed away. It was on a Thursday. I was able to visit her the Tuesday prior. It was a normal visit, sad as I think we both knew our time together on Earth was nearing the end, but it was a good visit. We talked as if it were any other visit, and just enjoyed each other's company one final time. I made plans to go see her the next day, but when I called her she said that she was tired and just needed to sleep. She passed away the next day, at her house, and as far as I knew she didn't suffer, and was in the least amount of pain as possible.

It was experiences like these, and others that I began to believe in the capabilities and the true presence of the Lord in the Eucharist at Adoration of the Blessed Sacrament, and also in the liturgy of the Catholic Mass. In the liturgy of the Catholic Mass we express our faith in the real presence of Christ under the species of bread and wine by, among other ways, genuflecting or bowing deeply as a sign of adoration of the Lord (CCC 1378)[1].

Eventually I also learned and began to understand that through the Rosary and Adoration, I would obtain everything I asked for, BUT only if it was compatible with the Lord's will, and if it was for the better benefit of my soul or the person's soul that I was praying for.

I learned also that just like it says in Ecclesiastes Chapter 3, Verse 1:

> *"There is an appointed time for everything, and there is a time for every event under heaven."*[5]

Including a time for birth.

On December 10, 2012, my brother Mike, and his wife Diana welcomed their new daughter, Lucy. She was born exactly 739 days after I began my first 54 Day Rosary Novena, asking the Blessed Mother to pray with me to ask God to bless my brother and his wife with a baby.

All of those Rosary prayers, and the prayers before while visiting Adoration of the Blessed Sacrament were not in vain. There really was a true presence of The Lord in the Eucharist. Finally, I learned that the Rosary prayers were compatible with the Lord's will, and Lucy truly is for the better benefit of my brother Mike's soul and his wife Diana's soul also. There really is an appointed time for everything, and there really is a time for every event under heaven. About a year and a half later, during Spring Break 2014, I was in Gloversville, and Mike, Diana, and Lucy were on vacation together in Myrtle Beach, South Carolina. My brother sent me a picture text message. It was a photo of the three of them, Lucy was wearing a pink shirt that said, "I'm going to be a big sister."

A couple of months after that, I was at The Magic Kernel in Johnstown, NY, and I got another picture text message from my brother. They were at the doctor's office. The picture that he texted me was an ultrasound picture, containing the words "Baby A" and "Baby B". Mike and Diana were now expecting twins, Lucy was going to have two younger brothers, due December of 2014.

About 18 months prior to receiving this announcement from Mike and Diana, the Feast of Corpus Christi was celebrated on June 2, 2013. On this day the Church celebrates the institution of the Eucharist. This day also celebrated the beginning of Perpetual Eucharistic Adoration by the Fulton-Montgomery County Deanery at the Church of the Holy Spirit in Gloversville, NY. According to the Catechism of the Catholic Church, because Christ himself is present in the sacrament of the altar, he is to be honored with the worship of adoration. "To visit the Blessed Sacrament is...a proof of gratitude, an expression of love, and a duty of adoration toward Christ our Lord." (CCC 1418)[1].

When Mike and Diana made the announcement that they were expecting again, I had already been one of the volunteers who helps make sure that Adoration of the Blessed Sacrament is exposed 24/7 at the Church and helping ensure that there is an Adorer there every hour of the day. The only time that Perpetual Eucharistic Adoration does not occur at the Church during the week is when Mass is being celebrated, or there is a funeral.

On September 16, 2014, I got a phone call from my brother Kolin around 5:30 in the evening. Mike and Diana were on their way to the hospital; Diana's water just broke, and they were rushing her to Albany Medical Center!

Immediately after hearing this, I went to the church, attended Adoration, and said a Rosary for Mike, Diana, and the twins, asking

the Blessed Mother to pray with me that everything would be OK that day for my brother, his wife, and the twins.
A few hours later, I got a call from my Mom that one of the twins was on his way, and they had to rush Diana into surgery.

Once again I came back to Adoration that night and I said another Rosary. There was another Adorer already there, I didn't know who it was at the time, but I later learned that his name was Gregg Wilbur. Before I started praying another Rosary for Mike, Diana, and the twins, I told Gregg that I had a family emergency and my phone might ring while I was there.

I was on the last Hail Mary bead when my brother Kolin texted me that the twins were born, both healthy, and both breathing mostly on their own. I turned to Gregg who was seated behind me at Adoration, and I told him what happened earlier, and told him about the news I just got from Kolin. Gregg said to me, "Oh my goodness, you're not going to believe this, but I have twin boys myself, they're both 8 years old now."

The next day, on September 17, I began another 54 day Rosary Novena asking the Blessed Mother to pray with me that the twins would come home from Albany Med NICU both happy, and healthy. 6 days after I finished that 54 day Rosary Novena, and exactly 60 days to the day after they were born, Mike and Diana were able to bring Jackson and Finley Hallenbeck home!

Eventually, once the twins were all home and settled, I got the opportunity to share this entire story with Diana; how I bought a Rosary for Grandma, then one for myself, and afterwards praying three 54 Day Rosary Novenas for Mike and her to have a baby. Immediately after I told her this entire story, she made the connection that she now has three kids, smiling ear to ear, the first thing that Diana said to me in reply was:

"Thank you for only saying three."

In closing, I have three things that I'd like everyone to remember and learn from this story.

1. Father Rendell was right back in 2011. Prayers before the Blessed Sacrament are very powerful. And when you pray

please remember that you will obtain what you ask for if it is compatible with the Lord's will, and if it is for the better benefit of your soul or the person's soul that you're praying for. In terms of the 54 Day Rosary Novena specifically, whether the prayer intention has been received or not after the first 27 days (3 Novenas), you must still say the 3 Rosary prayer Novenas (27 days) in Thanksgiving. Sometimes your prayers might be answered within 27 or 54 days, sometimes it could take 60 days or so, other times it might take 739 days, or maybe even longer. However long it takes for your prayers to be answered, please don't forget the capabilities and the true presence of the Lord in the Eucharist. Through the Rosary and Adoration, you will obtain everything you ask for, BUT again only if it is compatible with the Lord's will, and if it is for the better benefit of your soul or the person's soul that you are praying for. Lastly, as mentioned earlier: don't forget, "There is an appointed time for everything, and there is a time for every event under heaven." (ECC. 3:1).

2. On April 21, 2015 there was an article published on ewtnnews.com that told the story of a Nigerian Bishop named Bishop Oliver who was in his chapel last year at the end of 2014. The Bishop was in his chapel praying the Rosary before Adoration of the Blessed Sacrament when suddenly Jesus appeared. At first Jesus didn't say anything, but he extended a sword to the Bishop. Bishop Oliver reached for the sword, and as he went to grab it, the sword turned into a Rosary. Jesus then said to Bishop Oliver:

> "Boko Haram is gone. Boko Haram is gone. Boko Haram is gone."

In 2009 there was around 125,000 Catholics in Bishop Oliver's Dioceses in Nigeria, however after a surge of violence from the Islamist Extremist group called Boko Haram, today in 2015 there remains only 50-60 thousand Catholics left. It was clear to Bishop Oliver that what Jesus meant when he told him three times: "Boko Haram is gone." Jesus meant that with the power of the Rosary we would be able to expel Boko Haram.⁶

Please share this story from Nigeria with your friends, family, and parishes, and ask them to pray the Rosary with you for this petition that God, Jesus, and the Holy Spirit will help remove that dangers and persecution of Christians demonstrated by Boko Haram and ISIS. The Rosary that Bishop Oliver was praying, is the same one that you and I can pray also. If possible, I'd highly recommend praying the Rosary while attending Adoration of the Blessed Sacrament. Through praying the Rosary, attending Mass to celebrate the Eucharist, and visiting Adoration of the Blessed Sacrament not only will you have the opportunity to change your life, but together both you and I along with help from the Blessed Mother Mary can help change the world to make it a better place to live.

3. When you first started reading the inspirational story of the 54 Day Rosary Novena in Gloversville, NY, I told you that there were 3 things that I learned that stood out to me right after I bought my first set of Rosary beads.

> The first thing I learned was the Miraculous 54 Day Rosary Novena.
>
> The second thing I learned was the power of the Rosary and the Scapular working together.
>
> The third thing that I learned and that stood out to me, happened when I was reading Saint Louis De Montfort's excellent book, <u>The Secret of The Rosary.</u> Inside the cover of <u>The Secret of The Rosary</u> there is a quote from the Blessed Mother Mary to Saint Dominic, it reads:

"One day through the Rosary and the Scapular,

I will save the world.⁷

The story of the 54 Day Rosary Novena from Gloversville, NY is one that I wanted to share with you to exhibit events in my and my family's lives that portray special times involving prayer, a sacrament, and strengthened faith.

Today, right now, please make this moment a special time in your own life and begin praying the 54 Day Rosary Novena. Also if the opportunity is present in your area, I highly encourage you to pray the Rosary in the company of Adoration of The Blessed Sacrament.

Blessed Mother Teresa of Calcutta once said, "The time you spend with Jesus in the Blessed Sacrament is the best time you will spend on Earth. Each moment that you spend with Jesus will deepen your union with Him and make your soul everlastingly more glorious and beautiful in Heaven, and will help bring about everlasting peace on Earth."[8]

In 1884, when the Blessed Mother Mary gave to us the 54 Day Rosary Novena, it changed the lives of the Agrelli family in Naples, Italy when they were blessed with miracles for Fortuna's healing. 130 years later it changed the lives of my brother and his wife when they were blessed with miracles during the birth of their three children.

Now is your time to pray the Miraculous 54 Day Rosary Novena.

Through praying the 54 Day Rosary Novena, I hope that in the future it brings you joyful prayer, happiness through the sacraments, strengthened faith, and an abundance of blessings and miracles in your life.

What People are saying about...
The Miraculous 54 Day Rosary Novena to Our Lady

From amazon.com...

Perfect condition.

"This is a very good teaching tool for the rosary!"

-Christi J.
Verified Purchase
Reviewed in The United States
May 19, 2020

Easy to follow for the novice.

"Very clear and easy to follow, especially for those who have not memorized all the prayers."

-Marijane.
Verified Purchase
Reviewed in The United States
February 3, 2020

Truly a Miracle Novena!

"I had heard miracles from this novena, and after so many hints from Above I got the book. Just like I had heard, on the 28th day, which is the last day in the novena you're doing the prayers of petition, I had an answer to what I was praying for. My girls' dad has been out of their lives for 4 years, no child support, nothing. Lots of tears and heartbreak. And that day he called and said he wanted to make things right. He spent Thanksgiving with us, and has been helping financially and calls them every day. If you knew the awful back story you'd know how huge a miracle this is. Our Lady is so good to us! I just started a second round of it and I don't see myself stopping there when theres so many hurting people out there who need her intercession. T"

-Amazon Customer
Verified Purchase
Reviewed in The United States
December 4, 2019

From goodreads.com...

Samantha Thornberry rated it ★★★★★   Dec 24, 2019
Shelves: 2020

This book has greatly elevated my prayer life. I would recommend this book to any Christian/ Catholic trying to start the Rosary Novena. Such a great buy! I had never heard about the Rosary Novena until Ascension Presents talked about it on their YouTube channel! 54 days of a rosary is very rough you are pushing through it. I have integrated a prayer routine with it and have been loving the results. I would recommend this to anyone looking to dive deeper into faith with God!

From goodreads.com (Kindle version -<u>Rosary Novenas to Our Lady</u>)

Bice rated it ★★★★★   Mar 28, 2020

Finally!! Thank You Christopher!!
I have been praying the 54 Day Novena almost perpetually for several years. It consists of 27 Rosaries in Petition and 27 Rosaries in Thanksgiving. One prays one 5 decade Rosary daily in order : Joyful, Luminous, Sorrowful and Glorious. Then repeat sequence for a total of 27 Rosaries in Petition and 27 Rosaries in Thanksgiving. There are special prayers and virtues for each decade. I have several physical and Kindle booklets for the 54 Day Novena. They are good but one has to flip back and forth and keep track on paper on which Mystery one is praying on a particular day.
This book is genius! The Kindle edition has all the prayers and all the decades written out for each day in order 1 to 54 !! No more getting mixed up as to which Mystery one is praying. No more flipping back and forth. Lovely illustrations also. (The physical booklet I bought of same book of course can not duplicate this as it would be at least 900 pages long!)
Highly , Highly recommend praying the 54 Day Rosary Novena (Have received many graces.) and if you have a Kindle or even a Kindle App pray with this wonderful book. (less)

3 likes · Like · see review

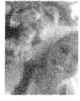

Samantha Thornberry rated it ★★★★★   May 12, 2020

Love this book! Praying the rosary was never one of my strong suits. However I am currently on my second Rosary Novena and it has been life changing. I have recently been trying to grow closer to God and taking a deep dive into Catholic and Christian literature has been amazing.

Great Rosary experience.

"Rosary at its fullest. You feel the power of our Blessed Mother praying for you from the begin to the end."
-Katrina Bell
Amazon.com - January 1, 2021

89

Meditating on The Rosary.

"My wife and i are meditating on the rosary everyday since we got hold of this book. We thanks the Virgin Mary of the guidance we are receiving from her intercession."

-Atong Tuson on Amazon.com
Verified Purchase. April 17, 2021

"I haven't done a 54 day rosary in years but was finding a need to. I needed guidance because it could get confusing after a while. Great tips in keeping track of the rosary, the prayers and the whole point of the devotion. I found it helpful and comforting to have this guidebook."

-Maureen Colsquared
goodreads.com
December 16, 2020

"I have a confession to make. I find praying the rosary boring. My mind wanders and even though it usually only takes 20 minutes it can feel like an eternity to me. I've been looking for books on the rosary that will help me become more invested in my prayer time. I love this book on praying the 54 Day Novena. A 54 day novena seems daunting but each day is mapped out with a specific intention to pray. The author, Hallenbeck, has even included the Luminous Mysteries which other books on the 54 Day Novena omit. There is a graph which shows the order in which to pray the novena, hint, it's not in the typical order designated by the day of the week. There is a picture for each mystery that you can use for reflection. I bought both the paperback book, including copies to give as gifts, and the kindle version. I prefer the kindle version because it goes straight through the rosary, day by day, without having to flip back and forth through the book. Others may prefer having the actual book in their hands. Even though I just marked this as finished reading today, I've actually worked through it twice in the last five months with the same special intention."

-Mary
goodreads.com
October 22, 2020

Totally exquisite and makes the enjoyment of the 54 day obvious and enjoyable.

"This book has helped so very much with the 54 day effort. Essential to any Catholic. A retreat, a place to go, and amazingly strengthening for full enjoyment of the 54 day Rosary."

> *- DamzelFly*
> *Amazon.com*
> *Verified Purchase, July 19, 2022*

Beautiful Novena!

"The author made this book super Easy to follow. Several extra daily prayers before and after the rosary. He did an excellent job putting it together for the ease of the rosary prayer warrior."

> *-MPH*
> *Amazon.com*
> *Verified Purchase, March 22, 2022*

Complete help to recite the prayerful novena.

"A great update to the 1954 novena booklet, it has the illuminous mysteries. I loved this so much, that ordered one for my sister-in-laws too. Thank you for updated the novena :)"

> *-Kathleen B.*
> *Amazon.com*
> *Verified Purchase, June 1, 2020*

Helpful and easy to use.

"A great book for this novena. I am 32 days into my 54 day novena and it's going very well. This is a very helpful book. I highly recommend."

> *-Elena*
> *Amazon.com*
> *Verified Purchase, May 30, 2020*

About Frank Morgan

Frank Morgan lived an incredible life. His obituary, *"F.J. Morgan, Architect, Dies at 78."* was originally published on Wednesday, August 6, 1969 in *The Troy Record* Newspaper, Troy, NY. It is an amazing, and impressive article, and it is available in its entirety on pages 96-100. Thank you for reading, and please pray for the resting of Mr. Morgan's soul.

Frank J. Morgan

"Our Lady of Mount Carmel, Roman Catholic Church" in Gloversville, NY. Original Architectural Drawing by Frank J. Morgan, Troy, NY

Frank J. Morgan working in an Orthodox Church.

F. J. Morgan, Architect, Dies At 78

Frank J. Morgan of 334 7th Ave., retired Troy architect, died Tuesday at Samaritan Hospital. Mr. Morgan had been in failing health for the last several months. He was 78.

Mr. Morgan practiced architecture in the Troy area for more than 30 years, specializing in ecclesiastical and school buildings. He designed numerous churches throughout the Albany Catholic Diocese during the late 20s and 30s and was especially devoted to carrying out Gothic detail.

He began his career as a draftsman and surveyor, working with the Vermont Marble Co. in Rutland, Vt., and later with the Canadian Pacific Railroad in Saskatchewan. He served his apprenticeship as an architect with the Troy firm of Edward J. Lowth and the New York City firm of Goodhue & Goodhue.

Founds Firm

In 1920, he started the architectural firm of Morgan & Milliman in this city and, after the death of his partner, Louis Milliman, in 1933, Mr. Morgan continued private practice until his retirement in the early 1960s.

During World War 11, he served as an architect on government projects in McComb, Miss.; Geneva and Scotia. He also served as consulting engineer for Behr Manning Corp.

Mr. Morgan was noted for his insistence on personally supervising all areas of construction, and for his careful research into historical background where related to any construction project. One of his designs, the chapel for the Sisters of the Good Shepherd in Troy, was featured in national architectural publications because of its unique structure, which made the main altar visible from a cloistered area as well as from the chapel whole.

Designed Shrine

Designed Shrine

Mr. Morgan was architect for the shrine of Cateri Tekawitha, North American Indian considered for canonization. Commissioned by the late Bishop Edmund F. Gibbons to design the shrine, Mr. Morgan visited Indian reservations in Canada so he could appropriately combine symbols of Indian lore and of Christianity in the building.

Among structures the late architect designed were St. Mary's Church, Hudson; the Carmelite Monastery, Schenectady; the Church of the Holy Spirit, East Greenbush; the altars of St. Peter's and St. Augustine's churches, Troy; Sacred Heart Church, Berlin; the Bishop's Chapel at Brant Lake; St. Patrick's School, Troy; the Masonic Temple, Troy; the Pioneer Building Loan and Savings Association; Troy High School, and Hoosic Valley Central School, Schaghticoke.

In addition to practicing architecture, Mr. Morgan operated a large dairy farm in Melrose from 1925 to 1941, raising Holstein cattle as a hobby. The farm was one of the few in this part of the state licensed to sell raw milk. In later years, he raised saddle horses and one of his horses won the national championship for Morgan stallions at the New England show in Northampton, Mass., in 1953.

Born in the Town of Pittstown, son of the late Patrick J. and Elizabeth O'Neil Morgan, he was educated at St. Augustine's Academy, graduating in 1907, and at Troy Business College. He later studied architecture at Columbia University and McGill University, Canada. He was admitted to practice as a registered architect in the State of New York in 1920. He served with the U.S. Army during World War I as a civilian at the Watervliet Arsenal.

He was a member of the Troy Rotary Club, the Troy Lodge of Elks, the Knights of Columbus, the American Institute of Architects, the Holstein-Freisan Association of America, and the Lansingburgh Historical Society. He also served on the advisory board of construction technology for Hudson Valley Community College. He was a communicant of St. Augustine's Church.

Survivors include his wife, the former Mary Weir of Troy; two sons, Frank J. Jr., dean of general studies at Hudson Valley Community College, and Paul J. Morgan, a Troy attorney; two daughters, Mrs. Charles Dumas of Albany and Sister Martha Daniels, C.S.J., of St. James Convent, Albany; one sister, Mrs. Leo Bouchard of Troy, and two grandchildren.

Funeral services will be at 8:15 a.m. Friday from the McLaughlin Funeral Home and at 9 a.m. from St. Augustine's Church where a Solemn Requiem Mass will be celebrated. Interment will be in St. John's Cemetery, Schaghticoke.

About The Author

Christopher Hallenbeck is a 4th Degree Sir Knight in Saint René Goupil Assembly #1427, and a 3rd Degree Brother Knight in Knights of Columbus Council #265 located in Gloversville, NY. Chris is an 11 time Past Grand Knight of Council 265, and also a Past Faithful Navigator of Assembly #1427. During the time he served as Grand Knight, Council 265 earned many awards in recognition of their service to the Catholic Church, the community, and also to The Knights of Columbus. He currently lives in Gloversville, NY.

Thanks and Acknowledgments

Thank you Mom, Mike, Kolin, Diana, Abbey. Thank you Olivia, Luciana, Connor, Jackson, and Finley - *you five are the best!* Thank you Mary Jo and Cubby Faville. Knights of Columbus Council #265. Bishop Ed Scharfenberger. Father Don Czelusniak. Father Rendell Torres. Father Matthew Wetsel. Father James Davis. Father Francis Vivacqua. Charles V. Lacey. The Adorers at the Perpetual Eucharistic Adoration Chapel at The Church of The Holy Spirit. Thank you Diana Hallenbeck, Melissa Faville Hally, Dr. Lana Mowdy, and Maren Kate Ruth for your editing and proofreading help. Esther Gefroh, owner of blogspot "A Catholic Mom in Hawaii" for permission to use her photo of the Our Lady of Fatima Statue. Dan Rudden, owner and operator of The Rosary Foundation, for permission to use the How to Pray The Rosary image. Thank you Gareth Bobowski. Thank you to the late Frank Morgan. Thank you to Sir Knight Greg Mattes and Thank You also to Mary Teresa Morgan. Mary's Grandfather, Frank Morgan, was the original architect of Our Lady of Mount Carmel Church (now Church of The Holy Spirit) in Gloversville, NY. In November 2019, I was introduced to Mary Teresa Morgan through SK Mattes while both were attending the Knights of Columbus Memorial Mass in Gloversville. This introduction was the first time that I learned of Frank's work, and it is how I received a copy of Frank's original architect drawing of the Church featured on the covers of this book.

Thank You for praying the Rosary.

A small request. If you enjoyed this book- if it helped you learn the Rosary, pray the Rosary, or if you were blessed. Could you leave a review on amazon.com please? Thank You! *"Together, let's promote the rosary. Together, let's change the world."–Chris*

END NOTES

1. <u>Catechism of The Catholic Church</u>. New York: Doubleday, 1994.

2. Lacey, Charles. <u>Rosary Novenas To Our Lady</u>. Woodland Hills: Benziger Brothers, 1926.

3. Johnson, Kevin Orlin. <u>Why Do Catholics Do That?: A Guide to the Teachings and Practices of the Catholic Church</u>. New York: Ballantine Books, 1994.

4. Sly, Randy. "Nine Days of Focused Prayer: What is a Novena?" *www.catholic.org* 14 May 2010

5. <u>The New American Bible</u>. Canada: World Catholic Press, 1987.

6. Holdren, Alan. "After vision of Christ, Nigerian bishop says rosary will bring down Boko Harem." *www.ewtnnews.com* 21 April 2015

7. Saint Louis De Monfort. <u>The Secret of The Rosary</u>. Charlotte: TAN, 1993.

8. "Eucharistic Adoration Quotes Blessed Mother Theresa of Calcutta" stfrancisadoration.org   30 May 2016.

Note:

"An Inspirational Rosary Novena Story from Gloversville, NY" was first published in:

Hallenbeck, Christopher. <u>The Miraculous 54 Day Rosary Novena to Our Lady: Daily Prayer Guide to Help You Finish the Miracle Novena</u>. Gloversville: Great Point Publishing, 2019.

Frank Morgan Obituary Source Info:

"F.J. Morgan, Architect, Dies at 78." The Troy Record. Troy, NY. 06 August 1969, Wednesday. Page 26. *www.newspapers.com/clip/36070348/obit-frank-j-morgan-snr-1969/* 1 November 2020.

Printed in Great Britain
by Amazon